Praise for Richard Haass's *Foreign Policy Begins at Home*

"Haass delivers a cogent picture of the world and supports it with sharp and precise arguments." —*Foreign Affairs*

"A must read for aspiring diplomats." —*American Diplomacy*

"Haass persuasively shows that the United States continues to be the indispensable nation. . . . Haass's writing style is straight-forward and uncluttered by jargon. My academic colleagues will not find reference to 'hegemonic transition theories' or 'postmodernism,' which makes the book much more accessible to a wider readership." —*National Interest*

"[Haass] argues brilliantly. . . . [His] prescription says charity starts at home." —*UPI.com*

"This informative, well-written book is a necessary addition to any collection providing either experts or citizens with new and rational discussion of America's place in the world today." —*Library Journal*

"Lessons learned from the recent past and presented thought-fully as a viable new course." —*Kirkus Reviews*

"Richard Haass has long been a keen observer of the US po-sition on the world stage, and his must-read book is no ex-ception. Haass rightly explains that if the United States is to continue fulfilling the leadership role it has had since World War II, our country must be more restrained in what it does abroad and put its house in order at home by defusing the looming fiscal debt bomb that threatens our national security and global standing." —James A. Baker, III

"A concise, comprehensive guide to America's critical policy choices at home and overseas. Richard Haass writes without a partisan agenda, but with a passion for solutions designed to restore our country's strength and enable us to lead."
—Madeleine K. Albright

"A perceptive diagnosis and common sense prescription for what ails us as a nation. It is a practical guide for those who believe America's continued global leadership is critical in the twenty-first century, but who believe it must be anchored in restoration at home and more effective use of all the tools of American foreign policy abroad." —Robert M. Gates

"Richard Haass is one of America's most insightful and experienced thinkers. In *Foreign Policy Begins at Home*, Haass explains why our ability to wield power and influence abroad will depend on our confronting pressing challenges at home. He offers a sobering look at the domestic policies that are undermining our international competitiveness—and a thoughtful roadmap for strengthening America's position on the global stage." —Michael R. Bloomberg

FOREIGN POLICY BEGINS AT HOME

The Case for Putting America's House in Order

Richard N. Haass

BASIC BOOKS
A MEMBER OF THE PERSEUS BOOKS GROUP
New York

Hardcover first published in 2013 by Basic Books,
A Member of the Perseus Books Group
Paperback first published in 2014 by Basic Books

Books published by Basic Books are available at special discounts for
bulk purchases in the United States by corporations, institutions, and
other organizations. For more information, please contact the Special
Markets Department at the Perseus Books Group, 2300 Chestnut
Street, Suite 200, Philadelphia, PA 19103, or call (800) 810-4145, ext.
5000, or e-mail special.markets@perseusbooks.com.

The Library of Congress has cataloged the hardcover as follows:
Haass, Richard.
   Foreign policy begins at home : the case for putting America's house in
order / Richard Haass.
     pages ; cm
   Includes bibliographical references and index.
   ISBN 978-0-465-05798-6 (hardcover)—ISBN 978-0-465-06596-7
(e-book) 1. United States—Foreign relations. 2. United States—Politics
and government. 3. World politics. 4. International relations. 5. Security,
International. I. Title.
   JZ1480.H32 2013
   327.73—dc23
                                                    2012049203
ISBN 978-0-465-07199-9 (paperback)
ISBN 978-0-465-03864-0 (paperback e-book)

10 9 8 7 6 5 4 3 2 1

Dedicated to Brent Scowcroft

CONTENTS

PART II

RESTORATION ABROAD 81

PART III

RESTORATION AT HOME 121

FOREWORD TO
THE PAPERBACK EDITION

Foreign Policy Begins at Home, published in May 2013, was premised on two themes. First, the United States was overreaching abroad, in particular in the greater Middle East, where it was trying to remake societies and, in the cases of Iraq and Afghanistan, relying heavily on a large, costly military presence to do so. And second, the United States was underperforming at home, in the process allowing many of the foundations of its power to weaken.

The book made the case for two adjustments. One was in the realm of foreign policy: to reduce the emphasis on nation-building and the greater Middle East more generally, recommending instead a focus on more traditional foreign policy tasks, including maintaining stability in the Asia-Pacific region, better integrating North America, and working to narrow the gap between global challenges and the rules and organizations designed to manage them. The other adjustment involved national security: to decrease somewhat the resources (be they economic, military, or the attention of policymakers) devoted to foreign policy and increase efforts directed to rebuilding the country's infrastructure, improving its schools, decreasing its debt, and increasing economic growth. To bring this about, the book called for a new US grand strategy of "Restoration" that would endeavor to restore the foundations of American power and the proper balances within and between both foreign policy and national security.

As the above suggests, foreign policy and national security, while often used interchangeably, are in fact quite different. It helps to think of national security as a two-sided coin. One side is foreign policy—what a country does abroad, be it diplomatic, military, or in some other realm. The other side is more internal or domestic—all that a country does (or fails to do) to strengthen its economy and society. A country's national security reflects what it is doing in both domains. Grand strategy is what a country does to advance its national security.

Now, a year later, both the assessments and the recommendations in the book appear largely valid. I would, however, add a third concern, one related to but different than both overreach abroad and underperformance at home. Call it underreach: the risk posed by what appears to be a growing lack of understanding by many Americans of the close relationship between the state of the world—how much stability, how much prosperity—and the state of the United States. The result is that isolationism is making something of a comeback.

Isolationism was discussed only briefly in the first edition. Like underperformance and overreach, it stems from within the body politic and crosses party lines. And as is the case with political dysfunction, it raises questions in the minds of others about American reliability, something that tends to lead friends to act more independently and foes more assertively.

Isolationism can be a deliberate strategy or the result of cavalier disregard for the implications of domestic policies for the US role in the world. It can be spurred, as well, by those who exaggerate the costs of what it takes to be effective in the world and the consequences of those costs for what needs doing at home, be it improving schools or infrastructure. The reality is that at or near current levels of spending on defense there is no guns versus butter tension in US national security; to the contrary, the United States can and should have its cake and eat it.

No matter what the inspiration, the emergence of modern isolationism is deeply troubling. The United States cannot thrive at home in a world of turmoil—and the world will move in the direction of turmoil absent consistent American leadership. This is not hubris but a statement of fact: order cannot be expected to just materialize, and no other country or group of countries has the capacity and commitment to bring it about. American foreign policy needs to begin at home, but it cannot end there.

Each of these three threats to American national security—overreach, underperformance, and underreach—is home grown, things we do to ourselves rather than have done to us. The biggest threat to US national security stems from the growing political dysfunction at the federal level. States, cities, and municipalities are in some instances doing better, possibly because local officials tend to be held accountable by residents for getting things done that visibly affect their lives, whereas members of Congress and at times presidents (in what can seem like distant Washington) often are rewarded for what it is they prevent. But certain things can only be done (or done at scale) at the federal or national level, so Washington's failures are the country's.

The sad truth is that many things have gotten worse over the past year. There was the sequester, the government shutdown, and finally the near default in October 2013. The sequester is bad public policy. It makes little distinction between spending that constitutes investment in the country's future (be it human or physical) and other spending that does not. The sequester also dampens domestic demand (by cutting back government spending) at a time the economy is growing at roughly half its post–World War II average. Finally, the sequester fails to tackle long-term entitlement obligations that will build significantly over the next decade as baby boomers retire and age in large numbers. The impact on the debt promises to be substantial starting later this decade and then much worse over time. Near-term reductions in annual deficits and the sort of budget accord reached in December 2013 do not alter this reality.

A far better approach to the budget would be one that increases spending in the short term on undertakings that qualify as investment while reducing entitlement obligations down the road. Realistic possibilities for reining in Social Security spending include revising the way inflation is calculated and increasing the age of eligibility; as for Medicare, reforms also include raising the age of eligibility and increasing co-payments. Ironically, the sequester (by reducing the deficit in the near term) may have made it more difficult to tackle the challenge of entitlement reform, giving the erroneous impression that the problem is not as severe as many have suggested. But the day of reckoning has only been delayed, and it is not that far off. Alas, building the needed bipartisan support for entitlement changes may be a bridge too far for the foreseeable future.

The result is that debt remains a major problem for the United States. It fuels a need for large inflows of funds from abroad, potentially giving others leverage over US policies. It could also force an increase in US interest rates if lenders conclude that the risk of default requires higher returns to offset them. Higher rates would require much higher payments on the debt, in the process crowding out other, productive uses for federal funds. Higher rates would also slow economic activity. The result would be a vicious rather than virtuous cycle. The case for gradual debt reduction, an argument central to the first edition of this book, remains compelling.

Getting the deficit and cumulative debt under control are not simply ends in themselves but also a means to an end, in that doing so would create conditions for higher levels of economic growth. US growth rates in recent years have hovered just below 2 percent; as noted above, this is about half the modern average. The result is stagnant household incomes and low levels of employment. (Unemployment statistics are not a good gauge as they can be artificially low if people give up looking for work.) There are some recent signs of progress. But sustained high-level growth is possible, and could come from a mixture of policies, including immigration reform, trade pacts that expand exports, corporate tax reform, lower individual income tax rates, limiting tax loopholes (tax expenditures), improving education, reducing onerous regulations, and infrastructure modernization. Again, the problem is less a lack of ideas or options than it is a lack of consensus and a willingness to compromise.

The government shutdown in October 2013 was less a matter of bad policy than it was questionable politics. Many Republicans were motivated by their opposition to the Affordable Care Act (ACA), or Obamacare. Opponents of the ACA are within their rights to work to amend or repeal it by vote; failing that, to work to elect individuals to office who share their views and who are prepared to support amendment or repeal. But the US government cannot function if opposition to specific laws brings the government to a standstill.

The near default (which would have been triggered by a refusal to raise the so-called debt ceiling) was odd, in that votes to raise the debt ceiling are not a mechanism for increasing spending but simply a device to pay for what has already been bought as a result of decisions on discretionary spending, entitlements, defense and national security, and taxation. But the uncertainty over what Washington would do unnerved a world that holds trillions of dollars in reserves and is dependent on the dollar as the de facto global currency. Many viewed this vote as a proxy for the willingness and ability (or lack thereof) of the United States to play a responsible global role.

Fixing what appears to be a broken political system is easier said than done for a host of reasons, in part because many of the forces and actors that have made it what it is tend to resist changes that promise to dilute their influence. But special interests that bring money and intensity to one side of an issue can be offset by interests that are prepared to commit as much in the way of resources and time on the other side. Some are trying to do just this in the realm of gun control. Reforms that bring about open primaries and take away the power from state legislatures to draw congressional districts (and give the power to nonpartisan commissions, as is the case in California) can lead candidates to appeal to the political center. And as we have seen countless times throughout history, presidents can make a difference by what goals they choose to make a priority and by how relentlessly they pursue them.

For now, though, the mixture of sequester, shutdown, and near default has had a rash of consequences. They slowed US economic growth; delayed the passage of comprehensive immigration reform, which by providing a home to the most talented entrepreneurs and workers would likely contribute to US competitiveness and growth; detracted from the appeal of the American political model at a time the United States was making great efforts to promote democracy in the world; and absorbed massive amounts of time and attention on the part of government officials, among other things rendering it impossible for President Obama to make a long-scheduled trip to

Asia, thus raising questions about the depth of the US commitment to the "pivot" to Asia, in many ways the signature foreign policy initiative of his first term.

Perhaps most important, what took place (and did not take place) in Washington raised new questions around the world about American reliability. Such questions did not arise in a vacuum. To the contrary, they were already acute in the aftermath of President Obama's ill-advised, eleventh-hour decision to request authority from Congress to use military force against the government of Syria in the wake of its having used chemical weapons. What made Obama's decision so troubling was that, as he himself acknowledged, he already possessed all the authority he needed, there was great precedent for not approaching Congress for such limited military action, and he had already established Syrian use of chemicals as a red line that would be met with a strong US response. Forfeited, too, was a chance to reinforce the norm against any use of weapons of mass destruction.

We have seen a move away from overreach in foreign policy as involves resources. All US forces were removed from Iraq and at most a modestly sized residual force will be left in Afghanistan. The US role in Libya ("leading from behind") was kept limited; the involvement in Syria's civil war is even more circumscribed. Indeed, the problem for US foreign policy in the Middle East is less one of overreach than it is the gap between objectives (which are often ambitious in calling for leaders to be ousted or democracy to be built) and what the United States is prepared or able to do to bring them about. My preference would be for scaling back goals; both regime change and democracy should be embraced with infinitely more caution. What has not been scaled back, though, is US emphasis on the greater Middle East. It was instructive that the president's address to the UN General Assembly in September 2013 mentioned little else. Secretary of State John Kerry has made the region his priority. The reality, though, is that US influence in the region is limited, particularly when it involves trying to shape the character of local political systems. Instead, US efforts should focus on frustrating proliferation and terrorists and on shoring up the security and stability of select friends.

It would be wise for the United States to do more in Asia, where its interests are greatest and where US ability to influence them happens to be considerable. Asia, home to many of the wealthiest and most powerful countries of this era, will much more than the Middle East determine the trajectory of this century. This judgment reflects both the nature of US aims (in Asia, it is to promote order between rather than within states) and the relevance of US tools (both diplomatic and military) for carrying out this task. There is some progress here, including a new commitment to negotiating a trans-Pacific trade accord. What is missing is consistent, high-level diplomatic involvement aimed at shaping the thinking and behavior of such local governments as China, Japan, and South Korea. The risk is that absent confidence in the United States, local actors will take matters into their own hands, something that would likely lead to increased Chinese influence in some instances and heightened tensions and chances of conflict in others.

Rebalancing foreign policy away from the Middle East and toward Asia is not all that needs doing. The gap between global challenges and the rules and institutions in place to manage them is large and getting larger. Many are well known and were written about in the original edition: trade, climate change, nuclear proliferation, humanitarian intervention. The phrase *international community* is often invoked, but in reality little such community exists.

Two issues, however, now merit additional treatment. Both derive from new technologies. The first is drones. Drones— remotely piloted vehicles, or RPVs for short—can be used for reconnaissance or strikes (for example, against individuals believed to be terrorists). The United States has used them quite frequently for both. And although there is evidence indicating that the number of strikes being carried out by the United States is down, there is also evidence that drone technology has proliferated and will only spread more (to both state and non-state actors) with time. Missing, though, are any rules governing their employment.

The second issue concerns the Internet. Within the United States, revelations about the National Security Agency (NSA) have triggered intense debate about the proper balance between individual privacy and collective security. What should the government be able to do and how should it be able to do it? There is no simple answer, although I would argue that the pendulum will need to swing in the direction of collective security given the evolving nature of the threat. It is essential, though, that there be adequate oversight by elected officials and, whenever possible, robust public debate.

The international dimension is if anything more complex and controversial. There are no rules regarding espionage (commercial and otherwise) or digital attacks. Nor is their agreement on whether content should in some instances be controlled and, if so, by whom. Again, the technology has far outpaced governance.

At one level the challenge is reminiscent of what was the case some seventy years ago at the dawn of the nuclear era. A new technology with enormous destructive potential had emerged, but there were no rules or arrangements for limiting its diffusion or use. What evolved were the concept of deterrence (and ways to bring it about) as well as ways of using diplomacy and arms control to slow or prevent both the vertical and horizontal proliferation of nuclear capabilities.

The challenge in the cyber domain is if anything more complex. The technology is evolving quickly—much more quickly than anything in the nuclear realm. And unlike the nuclear realm, where the political challenge involves at most a handful of actors, the number of state and nonstate actors, from private companies to terrorists and hackers to criminal cartels, is essentially unlimited. The challenge (in this case, akin to what exists in the nuclear space) is how to permit desirable uses of the technology and limit the undesirable, something that is extraordinarily difficult to do in practice. Given the importance of all things digital, efforts to set rules for governing cyberspace and maintaining an open, global Internet ought to be a priority.

I want to end with two points. Although both figure prominently in the book, they are worth repeating here because of their importance and because a number of readers of the original edition appeared unable or unwilling to understand them. First, to argue that foreign policy begins at home is not to embrace isolationism or in any way shirk from what this country should do beyond its borders. To the contrary, the United States will only be in a position to do substantial things in the world if it has the means. This in turn requires restoring domestic capacity and not squandering it on fool's errands. The good news is that the absence of a great power both intent on challenging the United States and able to do so gives the United States something of a respite and, with it, the ability to focus more on repairing itself.

Second, the United States is not in decline. To the contrary, it has many things going for it, including a relatively balanced demography, an energy transformation, and an ability to invent and exploit new technologies. The United States still possesses the world's largest economy and its most potent military. What is more, a hallmark of democratic, market-based societies is their innate ability to correct and adjust. What is at issue and open to question is whether the United States still retains sufficient capacity for correction and adjustment. This is a political question.

The stakes are large. No other country or groups of countries have the capacity, the experience, and the inclination to lead efforts to build global order. It is instructive and ironic that Xinhua, the official Chinese news agency, recently called for a de-Americanized world. But a de-Americanized Asia would be one in which Japan and South Korea would spend more on defense and possibly move to acquire nuclear weapons. It is hard to see how such a change would benefit China or anyone else. More broadly, the alternative to a US-led world is an unled world of growing disorder: more hardship and conflict, less freedom and prosperity. The only question is whether Americans will come together to see that this does not happen.

Introduction

This relatively short book is predicated on a consequential idea: The biggest threat to America's security and prosperity comes not from abroad but from within. The United States has jeopardized its ability to act effectively in the world because of runaway domestic spending, underinvestment in human and physical capital, an avoidable financial crisis, an unnecessarily slow recovery, a war in Iraq that was flawed from the outset and a war in Afghanistan that became flawed as its purpose evolved, recurring fiscal deficits, and deep political divisions. For the United States to continue to act successfully abroad, it must restore the domestic foundations of its power. Foreign policy needs to begin at home, now and for the foreseeable future.

Foreign Policy Begins at Home is a book that I never imagined writing. Sandpaper off the nuances and subtleties, and this is a book that argues for less foreign policy of the sort the United States has been conducting and greater emphasis on domestic investment and policy reform. For someone such as me, a card-carrying member of the foreign policy establishment for nearly four decades, this borders on heresy.

What got me to this point? More than anything else it began with the second Iraq war (begun in 2003) and the Afghan troop surge initiated in 2009. I mention both because my differences over the trajectory of American foreign policy are not with a single party. Many participants in the foreign policy debate in both parties appear to have forgotten the injunction of former president and secretary of state John Quincy Adams (that America "goes not abroad in search of monsters to destroy"), along with the lessons of Vietnam about the limits of military force and the tendency of local realities to prevail over global abstractions. As was the case with Vietnam, neither Iraq nor Afghanistan (as of 2009) was a war of necessity; more important, neither was a justifiable war of choice. In both cases, the interests at stake were decidedly less than vital. In both cases, alternative policies were available that promised outcomes of comparable benefit to this country at far less cost. And in both cases, history and even a cursory study of the societies in question suggested that ambitious attempts to refashion the workings and political cultures of these countries would founder. What is more, all this was predictable at the time. Now, with the advantage of hindsight, we can see that more than a decade of enormous sacrifice has hurt this country's reputation for judgment and competence and failed to produce results in any way commensurate with the human, military, and economic costs of the undertakings. Such an imbalance between means and ends makes no strategic sense at the best of times; it is even less defensible now, when the United States faces difficult challenges to its solvency.

This book grows naturally out of two previous books of mine. *The Reluctant Sheriff*, published in 1997 in the early years of the post-Soviet, post–Cold War era, argued the United States, at a time when it enjoyed extraordinary advantages and possibilities to influence other governments, risked squandering a unique chance to bring about lasting change in the world by aiming too low and trying too little in the way of erecting new international institutions able to contend with emerging global challenges. The second, published in 2005 and called *The Opportunity*, made the case that the United States was trying to do too much of the wrong thing (most notably, the 2003 Iraq war) and again argued for greater efforts to establish enduring international arrangements that would help tame globalization and curb the all-too-real economic and security threats to American interests and global order.

Where this book differs most from my previous books is in its focus on domestic policy, for remaking ourselves more than the world. There are, of course, external challenges, including but hardly limited to a rising China, a militarized North Korea, an Iran possibly moving to acquire nuclear weapons, an unstable Pakistan, violent terrorists, and a warming planet. These are real and justified concerns that warrant serious responses. But what makes the situation particularly worrisome are a large number of internal developments, including a burgeoning deficit and debt, crumbling infrastructure, second-class schools, an outdated immigration system, and the prospect for a prolonged period of low economic growth. Many of the foundations of this country's power are eroding; the effect, however, is not limited to a deteriorating transportation system or jobs that go unfilled or overseas owing to a lack of qualified American workers. To the contrary, shortcomings here at home directly threaten America's ability to project power and exert influence overseas, to compete in the global marketplace, to generate the resources needed to promote the full range of US interests abroad, and to set a compelling example that will influence the thinking and behavior of others. As a result, the ability of the United States to act and lead in the world is diminishing. I would prefer not to test the notion that this country requires a full-fledged crisis, be it in the form of a run on the dollar or some catastrophe brought about by terrorists or nature, to get its government to do what needs doing, in part because if it does, it will be that much more painful and expensive to address the shortcomings of America's economy, schools, immigration policy, infrastructure, and much more.

I write all this with the expectation I may well be caricatured on two fronts. One possibility is that I will be depicted as a defeatist, just another apostle of American decline. So let me be as clear as I can: I believe the United States enjoys great strengths and great potential. The US economy is the world's largest and is still growing; the best in American higher education is the best in the world; this society remains remarkably innovative and adaptive; its endowment of fresh water, energy, and arable land is nothing less than bountiful; and the population is relatively "balanced" in that it suffers from neither the bulges in young people nor old people that characterize so many other societies around the world. Recent breakthroughs in domestic oil and gas production thanks to new technologies and techniques are but the latest example of this country's ability to handle the significant challenges it faces.

But to say the United States is not in decline is something different from suggesting Americans ought to be sanguine with where they are and where they are heading. Given its considerable endowments and advantages, this country is clearly underperforming. Meanwhile, many other countries are performing better than they did in the past, and in some areas are doing better than the United States. The combination of these trends bodes poorly for the ability of the United States to compete economically and to shape international events.

I also anticipate being denounced as an isolationist. Isolationism is the willful turning away from the world even when a rigorous assessment of national interests argues for acting on their behalf. Isolationism makes absolutely no sense in the twenty-first century. Even if it wanted to, the United States could not wall itself off from global threats such as terrorism, nuclear proliferation, trade and investment protectionism, pandemic disease, climate change, or a loss of access to financial, energy, or mineral resources. Borders are not the same as barriers. The US government must be active in addressing these threats. There are also opportunities to be had, including the possibility of lifting hundreds of millions and potentially billions of people out of poverty, increasing the quality of life as well as life expectancy, expanding individual freedom, and settling disputes before they lead to armed conflict. Embracing isolationism would accelerate the emergence of a more disorderly and dangerous world, one that would be less safe, less free, and less prosperous. Isolationism would be folly.

At the same time, the United States must become significantly more discriminating in choosing what it does in the world and how it does it. Hard choices need to be made. It is not simply that it needs to recognize that the limits to its resources require it to be exacting in setting priorities; it must also recognize the limits to its influence. The United States needs to rethink what it seeks to accomplish abroad. Americans must distinguish between the desirable and the vital as well as between the feasible and the impossible. For the past two decades, American foreign policy, consumed with remaking large parts of the greater Middle East, has quite simply overreached. There is a strong case to be made that US attention and efforts should be better distributed around the world, with greater focus on the increasingly critical Asia-Pacific region and the Western

Hemisphere and somewhat less on the Middle East; there is an even stronger case that US foreign policy should focus not so much on what other countries *are* within their borders and more on what they *do* outside their borders. This will be difficult at times, as situations will arise in which standing aside will appear to be immoral or strategically shortsighted or both; that said, the United States needs to balance its desire to do good with its ability to do good—as well as with the need to do many other things on behalf of its citizens at home and its interests abroad.

To mount an effective foreign policy the United States must first put its house in order. The most obvious reason is resources. National security does not come cheap. Money—lots of it—is required to field a capable modern military with a broad range of missions, to generate necessary intelligence against a broad range of threats, to protect the homeland against a broad range of contingencies, to carry out diplomacy and dispense assistance to promote a broad range of interests. The United States now spends close to $800 billion a year on these tasks—roughly one-fifth of all federal spending and some 5 percent of total GDP. The economy must grow at traditional rates (near or above 3 percent) and domestic spending that does not qualify as investment must be kept in check if this country is not to be forced to choose between national security and all else. Alas, the US economy is now growing at only half this rate, while domestic spending that has nothing to do with investment is rising.

The United States is far more likely to find itself threatened and attacked if it is perceived to be weak and vulnerable. A strong United States will discourage would-be competitors or adversaries from going down the path of confrontation. A strong United States would make others more likely to work with it than against it. And a strong United States would be better able to deal with any foe that miscalculated.

The United States must also put its house in order if it is to avoid placing itself in a position of high vulnerability to forces or actions beyond its control. Right now the US government requires an inflow of more than $1 billion a day to support a gross federal debt that stands at about $16 trillion and increases by more than $1 trillion a year. We can look to our own history to see what can happen when foreign governments obtain this kind of leverage. In 1956, the US government, furious over Great Britain's participation in the invasion of Egypt after Nasser's nationalization of the Suez Canal, blocked international loans the British needed to avert a collapse of their currency. The British government of the day was forced to back down. Now imagine what might happen were China to threaten a similar action against the United States amid a crisis over Taiwan or the South China Sea.

Another scenario is simply one in which money markets lose confidence in America's ability to manage its own finances and start to exact a higher price for their continued willingness to lend money. This would force the Federal Reserve to raise interest rates, not for the traditional purpose of cooling inflationary pressures, but rather to attract needed dollars that demand a higher return given concerns over American credit-worthiness. This would spell disaster for an economy barely out of recession. This scenario might have come to pass already had it not been for the Eurozone crisis, which removed a viable alternative to the dollar. But Americans cannot count on Europeans to forever do the wrong thing, or on China's remaining unwilling to allow its currency to take on an international role.

Then there is the power of example. A successful American economy, one that is generating wealth and jobs and innovation, along with a successful American political system and society, one that is willing and able to take difficult but necessary decisions, presents not just the image but the reality of a country functioning at a high level, one with political freedom, a high and rising standard of living, and social mobility. This is a model other countries will want to emulate. The battle of ideas is far from over; indeed, it has grown more intense with the economic success of China and other authoritarian regimes, with the difficulties experienced by the mature democracies in 2008 and subsequently, and with the dramatic developments that have taken place across the Middle East starting in late 2010. Foreign policy is not just about what diplomats say and soldiers do: It is also about the example a country sets.

It is also true that a more effective foreign policy would redound to the benefit of Americans at home, with more resources to be spent on and in their society, be it by individuals or the federal, state, and local government to enhance the quality of life, standard of living, or security. A more peaceful and organized world would create conditions in which the American economy should thrive. And a thriving economy—one growing at relatively robust levels—will improve the lot of most Americans. This is important, as tolerance for income and wealth inequality tends to be greater if everyone's situation is improving. Absent such growth, social and economic mobility will atrophy and class frictions will increase, leaving the population focused inward.

It is not too late for the United States to put its house in order. It is not simply a case of necessity; currently it has an extraordinary opportunity to do so. The world is a relatively forgiving place now and for the foreseeable future. There is no twenty-first-century equivalent to what Germany was in the first half of the twentieth century and the Soviet Union was in the second. Of course, there are actual and potential threats to American interests and well-being, but none rises to the existential. China could in theory come to challenge the United States for primacy, but it is far from assured that it will have the means and the appetite to do so. In any event, and as will be discussed, any such challenge is neither inevitable nor imminent. The United States is fortunate to have something of a strategic respite; how long-lasting and extensive it will be will, of course, depend in part on the decisions and actions of others. But even more it will depend on how successful the United States proves to be at repairing the foundations of its power, how disciplined it can be at wielding that power, and how wise it is in providing others an incentive to share in the building and operating of the international order.

This book is divided into three parts. The first focuses on the world, on the principal features of the international system a generation after the end of the Cold War, just over a decade after 9/11, and half a decade after the onset of the American and then global economic crisis. The picture is one of American primacy—first among unequals, if you will—but also one of widely diffused power and technology in a world lacking in mechanisms for dealing with most of the challenges that already exist or soon will; a world in which some regions show far more dynamism than others; an era in which it is often difficult to translate power into influence; and a time in which governments are finding it hard to manage at home and cooperate abroad.

The second part of the book is more prescriptive, focusing on what the United States should and should not do abroad. The theme is one of a more discriminating foreign policy, both in what is sought and what is spent, complemented by a more disciplined domestic policy. The book will argue for the adoption of a new American foreign policy, one defined by a doctrine that would bring to an end an era characterized by large land wars designed to refashion countries in the greater Middle East, and replace it with an approach to the world that would place greater emphasis on the Asia-Pacific and Western Hemisphere, on instruments of statecraft other than the military, and on shaping more how other governments act beyond their borders rather than within.

The book's third part is also mostly prescriptive, but focuses on how America should tackle its internal challenges. The recommendations address the budget, energy, education, infrastructure, and immigration. The book also suggests economic policies that, if adopted, should stimulate growth, and political reforms that, if introduced, would make it more likely that the country's leaders would, or at least could, do what needs doing.

The stakes are enormous. The world will not sort itself out absent US leadership. This is not a call for unilateralism, which in most instances is not a viable option. Nor is it a reflection of American arrogance. It is simple fact. No other country has the capacity, habits, and willingness to take on this responsibility. Without such a benign force, order never just emerges. No invisible hand is at work to sort out the geopolitical marketplace. The question is whether the visible hand of the United States will be up to the challenge. One sincerely hopes for this to be so, as nothing less than the future of this country and the character of the twenty-first century are in the balance.[1]

Part I

The Return of History

"Tear down this wall" was Ronald's Reagan's terse message to Mikhail Gorbachev on June 12, 1987. Two and a half years later, Reagan's wish became reality. Optimism filled the air, not just in long-divided Germany and Europe, but throughout much of the world. History had ended, some argued: The age-old struggle between democratic capitalism and state authoritarianism had been settled once and for all.[1] The bipolarity that had dominated international relations during the four decades of Cold War, along with the multipolarity that had characterized the world for centuries before that, had given way to unipolarity, to an era of American dominance.[2] The world would be a largely benign place, and the American people, who had struggled and sacrificed for four decades of Cold War, could expect a hard-earned and well-deserved peace dividend.

More than two decades later, such optimism is mostly gone. The post–Cold War era has been turbulent. It began with the Iraqi invasion of Kuwait, a classic case of state-on-state aggression that might never have happened during the Cold War if only because the Soviet Union, Iraq's principal patron at the time, would not have permitted it lest it give the United States an opening to dispatch military forces to a critical region. This was followed by a series of civil wars and mostly internal crises in such countries as Somalia, the former Yugoslavia, and Rwanda. Humanitarian intervention—where and how to do it—seized center stage. The attacks of 9/11 were a shock, one that graphically demonstrated American vulnerability. Soon after came two costly, inconclusive wars in Iraq and Afghanistan that made many Americans skeptical of international involvement and question whether American military advantages could be translated into lasting gains that would justify the larger-than-expected costs. The hoped-for peace dividend never materialized.

At the same time, America's economic situation sharply deteriorated. As a result of massive domestic spending, steadily growing entitlements, sharply higher defense outlays, and increased interest on the debt, gross federal debt increased from $3.5 trillion at the end of the Cold War to some $16 trillion— approximately the size of the US economy in a single year—by 2012. The financial crisis of September 2008 provoked debates as to whether modern societies were able to effectively administer their own economies. Suddenly, the "Washington Consensus" and its preference for market-led economic development was out of fashion, replaced more and more by a model found in many Asian countries that emphasized a stronger role for the state.[3] Protests throughout Europe and inaction in the United States in the face of an enormous and mounting debt raised the related issue of whether today's democracies can make tough choices to prevent special interests from continuing to overwhelm the collective, national interest.

Optimism made something of a comeback in early 2011, when events in Tunisia, Egypt, and elsewhere in the Middle

East made many believe that positive political change was finally coming to a part of the world that had mostly missed out on the great democratic and economic revolutions (not to mention the Enlightenment) that had so transformed much of the former Soviet Union and large parts of Eastern and Central Europe, Asia, Latin America, and Africa. Now the optimism appears premature: ousting authoritarian regimes was one thing; replacing them with something demonstrably and enduringly better, quite another. Talk of an Arab Spring came to be replaced with the more neutral phrase "Arab upheavals," and, in some quarters, with references to an Arab Fall or even Winter.

What is surprising is that any of this surprises. History is always a struggle between competing ideas about how best to organize governments and societies and, at the international level, between forces of order and disorder. While the specifics differ from one era to the next, what does not change is the basic notion of ongoing competition between what the international relations theorist Hedley Bull termed forces of society and anarchy.[4]

The twenty-first century is no exception to this pattern. Numerous forces, including economic interdependence, which gives countries strong incentives to seek and maintain mutually beneficial economic relationships, are pushing the world toward order. Modern conflict between developed countries has the potential to be so destructive and costly that few differences justify recourse to war. Regional and global frameworks and organizations set rules, resolve at least some disputes, and offer a venue for consultations and negotiations on issues ranging from trade to arms control. There is as well the willingness and ability of responsible governments to threaten or employ physical force or other forms of pressure such as sanctions to prevent or discourage others from violating the established rules of order.

But then numerous forces of disorder, some unique to our modern world, also exist. These include the spread of nuclear weapons and materials and, in some cases, delivery systems to states and others; the actions of terrorists, pirates, and drug merchants; climate change; natural viruses that cause pandemic disease and those of the man-made variety that cause havoc with computers and the systems they operate; protectionism and other barriers to the relatively free flow of goods, services, and investment; and markets that on occasion cause great dislocation. We are also seeing the rise and decline of major powers, the challenges of aggressive medium-size countries, such as North Korea and Iran, and the vulnerability of weak or failed states that can easily become fertile ground in which the various manifestations of globalization's dark side tend to flourish.

Beginning to emerge are the outlines of a new era that resembles less the twentieth century than the nineteenth. Ours is a world of constant flux, shifting alignments, numerous power centers, and states coming together and apart—all with an overlay of modern technology and globalization. The potential for disorder is considerable, and will only be ameliorated through the concerted efforts of many of the world's most powerful countries led by the United States, the only country now and for the foreseeable future with both the capacity and the tradition of working on behalf of broader global arrangements to the benefit of others as well as itself. The question is whether the United States will continue to be that country, something that will require discipline in what America does at home and wisdom in what it does abroad. History, with some decidedly modern wrinkles, has returned if in fact it ever departed.

such countries as Germany, Great Britain, France, Turkey, Italy, and Poland stand out. Add to the mix those countries (often blessed with massive energy resources) that are accumulating enormous amounts of foreign exchange; which is to say, sovereign wealth. A good many organizations would be on the list, including those that are global (the UN, International Monetary Fund, World Bank), regional (the Organization of American States, the African Union, the EU, NATO, the Association of Southeast Asian Nations, the Arab League, and many others) and functional (including OPEC, the World Health Organization, the International Energy Agency, and the Shanghai Cooperation Organization). So, too, would be state governments (California in the United States, Uttar Pradesh in India) and cities (New York, Shanghai, São Paulo). Then there are the large global companies, such as JPMorgan Chase, Exxon Mobil, Apple, and Caterpillar, which dominate the worlds of finance, energy, technology, and manufacturing. Others deserving inclusion would be global media outlets (BBC, CNN, Al-Jazeera), militias (Hezbollah, Hamas), political parties, religious institutions and movements, terrorist organizations such as al-Qaeda, drug cartels, and nongovernmental organizations (NGOs) of a more benign sort—the Gates Foundation, Doctors Without Borders, Greenpeace, and Conservation International. Clearly, these countries and organizations do not possess the same kind or equal amounts of influence. But what distinguishes this era is the sheer number and variety of entities with global reach.

Many of those with influence are not nation-states. Indeed, one of the cardinal features of the contemporary international system is that nation-states have lost their monopoly and, in some domains, their preeminence. States are being challenged from above by regional and global organizations, from below by militias, cartels, and the like, and from the side by NGOS and corporations. Power is also dispersed in networks, markets, and exchanges, financial and otherwise.

Two factors—globalization and technology—contribute to nonpolarity. Globalization's central effect is to increase the volume, velocity, and importance of flows within and across borders of just about everything, including people, ideas, e-mails, greenhouse gases, viruses (computer and real), drugs, dollars, manufactured goods, television and radio signals, weapons, and a good deal else. Globalization is a defining feature of this era, differentiating this period from previous ones. It is a reality, not a choice. Our choice is how governments and other entities react to it.

Globalization reinforces nonpolarity in important ways. Many cross-border flows take place outside the control or even knowledge of governments. By definition, then, globalization dilutes the control of authorities of all countries. Second, these same flows often strengthen the capacities of many actors, be they energy exporters (which are experiencing a dramatic increase in wealth, owing to transfers from importers), terrorists (who use the Internet to recruit and train, the banking system to move resources, and the transport system to move people), outlaw or rogue states (which can exploit black and gray markets) or Fortune 500 firms (which quickly move personnel, investments, and instructions). It is easier than ever before for individuals and groups to accumulate and project substantial power.

The world is now experiencing a surprising growth of nationalism: Surprising, because nationalism was in many ways a central dynamic of the nineteenth and twentieth centuries; that it had largely been satisfied through widespread statehood or overtaken by regionalization and globalization was easy to assume. But the lure of statehood still exists for many of those minorities who do not have a country of their own. What is more, nationalism is making something of a comeback as the ability of existing governments and regional and global organizations to satisfy the desires of citizens comes up short. We are seeing signs of exactly this throughout the world: In Europe, national governments are often resisting the preferences of Brussels at a time when several of these same governments must contend with separatist movements within their borders; in China, popular pressures are increasingly driving and constraining the foreign policy of the government; in the Middle East and Europe, the resurgence of nationalism not only increases the potential for conflict between states but is leading to demands to create new ones. Nationalism also remains strong in the United States. Anyone doubting this need only consider the frequent references to American exceptionalism and the widespread mistrust of multilateralism and international institutions.

The other factor that reinforces the diffusion of power is technology. George Orwell's vision of the year 1984, with societies centrally controlled, could hardly have been more wrong. The hallmark of modern technology is decentralization. More computing power can now be held on a desktop or in a person's hand in the form of a smart phone or tablet than could be gathered in a room only a generation ago. Individuals and groups are empowered as never before.

People everywhere now have more access to more sources of information; it is harder and harder for governments to control, much less monopolize, its flow. The number of radio and television options has exploded, thanks to satellites and cable. Worldwide, there are some six billion cell phone subscribers; more than 100 million tablets of one sort or another are being produced and purchased each year; and one of every three people is now using the Internet.[1] Whatever their locale, individuals have a growing ability through mobile phones and social networking to communicate directly and discreetly with one another. A consequence of this trend is that it is more difficult for authoritarian governments to exert control over their citizens. The advance of technology is one explanation for the uprisings taking place in much of the Arab world. But modern technology has implications even for well-established democracies. It is far more difficult to generate consensus and to govern in a world in which citizens have a wide range of choice when it comes to what they read, watch, listen to, and with whom they talk. Lack of consensus at home tends to make it more difficult for leaders to do what is often necessary, including compromise and committing resources, to cooperate abroad.

Nonpolarity will make it more difficult for the United States to fashion collective responses to regional and global challenges. With so many more actors possessing meaningful power and trying to assert influence, it will be more difficult to build consensus and make institutions work. In general, the more decision makers, the more difficult to make decisions. It is not simply that herding dozens is harder than herding a few; it is also that greater numbers make it far more likely that important actors may actively oppose what others do or want. The inability to reach agreement in the Doha round of global trade talks, or in various settings meant to address global climate change, are telling examples of just this.

Nonpolarity also increases the number of threats and sources of vulnerability to a country such as the United States, given its many global ties and transactions as well as its intrinsic openness. These threats can take the form of rogue states, terrorist groups, energy producers that choose to reduce their output, or central banks that, by what they do and fail to do, can create conditions affecting the strength of the dollar.

Iran is another case in point. Its progress toward becoming a nuclear power both reflects and reinforces nonpolarity. Thanks to the surge in oil prices and the removal of Iraq as a balancer, Iran has become a potent actor, one able to exert influence in Iraq, Lebanon, Syria, the Palestinian territories, and beyond. It has many sources of technology and finance, and numerous markets for its energy exports. Iran also underscores nonpolarity in that the United States alone cannot manage it but, to the contrary, is dependent upon others to support political and economic sanctions or block Iranian access to nuclear technology and materials.

This discussion is not meant to be fatalistic. Nonpolarity is inevitable, but its character is not. A great deal can and should be done to shape a nonpolar world. That said, order will not just emerge. Rather, left to its own devices, a nonpolar world will become messier and more violent over time. Think entropy, in which systems consisting of a large number of actors tend toward greater randomness and disorder absent concerted external intervention.[2]

American Primacy

Lost in the emotionally laden territory between "We're number one" and "We've lost it" is a country that still matters far more than any other. Even as the number of contenders has multiplied, and despite the reality that the United States no longer dominates as it once did, it remains, by most relevant measures, the most powerful and influential force in the world.[1] Appreciating the implications of this difference between being "the world's only superpower" and "first among unequals" is crucial.

The United States boasts the world's greatest economy; its annual GDP of $16 trillion is one-fourth of global economic output. This compares to $7 trillion for China and $6 trillion for Japan. Per capita GDP in the United States is close to $50,000, some nine times that of China.

The United States possesses the world's most capable military. No other country can come close to competing with it on modern battlefields. US core defense spending (not including what is spent on operations in active theaters such as Afghanistan) is slightly more than $500 billion, an amount greater than those of the next ten countries combined.

And then there is America's considerable diplomatic and cultural influence. The former stems in large part from its economic and military might, from the large US role in international organizations, and from American diplomatic activism. Cultural impact results from American television and films, world-class institutions of higher education that are a magnet for the best and brightest from around the world, and the experience many people have when they visit this country. Closely associated to American influence is the historic appeal of the American political, economic, and social model; by what it is and what it does, the United States often has been a catalyst for reform around the world.

But it is also true that the United States enjoyed in the 1990s a degree of advantage and influence that had few if any historical precedents. Thanks to the perception that it had won the Cold War, its booming economy, an absence of great power rivals, diplomacy that was often deft and disciplined, and military advantages that lent themselves to classic battlefield wars, the United States was able to help bring about not just German unification but German membership in NATO, NATO's subsequent enlargement, the eviction of Iraq from Kuwait, and the Madrid peace conference, the first ever face-to-face meeting between Israel and the relevant Arab governments for the purpose of negotiating peace.

So what has changed? On one level, not all that much. Even at the height of its strategic advantage in the post–Cold War years, the United States couldn't bend the world to its will and, then as now, depended on others in important ways, be it for diplomatic and military support, energy, markets, or cash. No amount of American diplomacy succeeded in bringing peace to the Middle East or consensus on what to do when governments attacked (or could not prevent large-scale attacks on) their own citizens. Talk of a unipolar world was just that: talk.

But something else was going on. Other countries—often with US encouragement and support—got better at producing and piecing together the human, financial, and technological resources that lead to productivity and prosperity. China's GDP increased from less than $400 billion in 1981 to more than $7 trillion three decades later; India's increased from under $300 billion to nearly $2 trillion over that same period. This rise of countries, along with that of corporations and other entities with meaningful power, cannot be stopped or even materially affected. The United States was growing and enjoyed a position of absolute primacy, but its position relative to others was unavoidably diminishing as other countries (which had the advantage of starting from a lower base) were gaining ground.

There is also a difference between military advantage and the ability to translate such advantage into enduring results. One lesson drawn by many parties from the one-sided outcome of the 1990–1991 Gulf War was that it was a fool's errand to challenge the United States militarily in wide-open spaces where it could bring its most modern and capable technologies and weapon systems to bear. Some governments such as North Korea and Iran that were concerned about a possible US military attack accelerated their development of nuclear weapons. Other governments (Iraq, for one) focused on developing the capacity for deploying irregular forces in built-up areas, a capacity that frustrated US efforts to assert order in the aftermath of Saddam Hussein's ouster. The result was a reduction in actual US military advantage. What matters is not the quantity and quality of all US military forces but the quantity and quality that can be brought to bear in particular circumstances. Often just a small percentage of US might comes up against all of what an adversary can muster, in part because the adversary is fighting on its own ground, and also because what is one square on the geopolitical chessboard for the United States constitutes the entire chessboard for a smaller country. The United States simply has too many interests and too many obligations to put all or even most of its eggs in any single basket.

Terrorism is another manifestation of the reality that military advantage does not translate into obvious security. The United States is a relatively open society, and with such openness comes vulnerability. This is one lesson of 9/11. Intelligence and law enforcement capabilities in this realm tend to be more relevant than military might; US defense forces play a secondary role at most. The fact that al-Qaeda was incomparably weaker than the United States was unrelated to its ability to inflict great harm on the cheap.

But other explanations for the deterioration in the relative position of the United States are home grown. To paraphrase Pogo, the character of Walter Kelly's comic strip popular a half-century ago, Americans have met the explanation, and, to a large extent, are it. Both by what it did and what it failed to do, the United States has accelerated the emergence of alternative power centers in the world and weakened its position relative to them.

Energy policy (or the lack of one) was one important driver behind this deterioration in the US posture. Following the first oil shocks of the 1970s, American consumption of oil nonetheless grew by some 20 percent, while imports more than doubled in volume and rose by 75 percent as a share of consumption. US oil consumption increased from just over 16 to nearly 21 million barrels a day between 1975 and 2005. American oil production failed to keep up, declining from 8.4 to 5.2 million barrels a day over that same period.[2] This US demand for imported oil helped drive up the world price significantly. The result was an enormous transfer of dollars and leverage to such countries as Saudi Arabia, Iran, Iraq, Libya, Qatar, Venezuela,

Nigeria, the UAE, and Russia, all of which became far wealthier and, in some cases, more powerful than they otherwise would have been.

Foreign policy also played a role in the weakening of America's position in the world. The Iraq war initiated in 2003 is a case in point. The United States did not have to go to war with Iraq. Saddam Hussein's Iraq was not involved in the 9/11 attacks and had little tradition of supporting terrorism. There were other options even if Iraq possessed (as my colleagues in the US government and I thought at the time) biological weapons and a desire to one day restart its nuclear program in earnest. In particular, sanctions could have been strengthened; deterrence was working and could have continued to work. Such arguments were overwhelmed by those who maintained it was essential to eliminate Saddam's thought-to-be considerable and sure-to-grow inventory of weapons of mass destruction. This conflict was expected to be a relatively quick and easy affair that would demonstrate to the world that post-9/11 America was back; further, that the much-changed Iraq that would result would spur democratic revolutions throughout the Middle East. All of these arguments prevailed—and all were proven wrong. It was an expensive lesson. Iraq proved to be an extraordinarily costly war of choice—in human, military, economic, and diplomatic terms. More than forty-four hundred American troops gave their lives; another thirty thousand suffered casualties.[3] The direct economic cost was on the order of $1 trillion, but, in reality, it will be far higher once long-term medical costs and lost productivity on the part of those killed or injured are factored in.[4] The immediate adverse strategic consequences of the Iraq war included Iran's emergence as a regional power no longer offset by a hostile Iraq and a much-damaged US reputation for everything from competence to respect for human rights. Another unfortunate result was the conclusion drawn by most Arab monarchs and leaders that democracy was to be resisted no matter what lest it lead to an outbreak of sectarian politics and chaos.[5]

What is more, the initial results of an Iraq run by Iraqis are less than encouraging. To be sure, there have been a number of relatively fair elections and political life is active. The economy is growing. Oil production is up. But a political culture of compromise has not taken root, and the country continues to be divided by geography, ethnicity, religion, and politics. There is no consensus on how to share the potential wealth from Iraq's vast energy resources. The Kurdish north is largely autonomous; where its writ ends and that of the central government begins is unresolved. Iranian influence is pervasive; Iraq's willingness to allow Iran to use Iraqi airspace and territory to supply arms and oil to a Syrian government that is killing thousands of its own citizens is hardly the expected return on American investment. Iraq still experiences regular terrorist bombings. Millions of Iraqis are either internally displaced or refugees. While certainly better in some ways than it was five years ago, present-day Iraq is far from a model that other countries will want to emulate. Few military interventions prove immune to the law of unintended consequences.

Afghanistan, which has earned the dubious distinction as America's longest war, has also proven extremely costly. More than two thousand American soldiers have lost their lives; close to twenty thousand have been injured.[6] The financial cost is already roughly $500 billion.[7] It didn't have to be that way. This is not to question the original decision after 9/11 to oust the Taliban government that had provided support to al-Qaeda; it was both justifiable and necessary to prevent further terrorist use of Afghanistan as a base to launch additional attacks against the United States. In addition, removing the regime in Kabul was meant to discourage other governments from carrying out terrorist acts or aiding those who did. Indeed, what the United States conducted in Afghanistan in the aftermath of 9/11 was a classic war of necessity: There was no other option that could accomplish what needed doing to protect vital US national interests in the time available.

What proved particularly consequential (and, I would argue, ill-advised) was the determination in 2009 to effectively triple US force levels and target not just al-Qaeda in Afghanistan but the Taliban. These decisions, built in part on policies introduced a year before by the previous administration, wrongly assumed Taliban gains automatically translated into gains for al-Qaeda and overlooked other options for dealing with al-Qaeda if it did reestablish itself in the country—drones and special forces come to mind—as well as the reality that, given its ethnic links, the Taliban would ultimately make major inroads in southern Afghanistan no matter what the United States did. A war of necessity morphed into a war of choice; in the process, the United States became a de facto protagonist in Afghanistan's civil struggle, when lesser options could have protected core US interests.[8] Making matters worse were ambitious goals for building a large military and creating police forces loyal to the Afghan state, objectives that mostly ignored the tradition of a weak central government.

What the United States will have to show for more than a decade of sacrifice and investment in Afghanistan will be minimal. It is difficult to be optimistic about the country's prospects in light of Taliban resilience, the weakness and corruption that plague Afghanistan's government, and the reality that Pakistan will continue to be a sanctuary for the Taliban and other armed groups that seek to gain a foothold or more in Afghanistan.

Much easier to foresee is an Afghanistan that will steadfastly remain the country it had been before a decade of enormous American involvement.[9]

Both of these wars represent graphic evidence that power in the abstract and the ability to influence particular situations are two very different things. The latter depends on the immediate balance of power; the relative degree of commitment of the parties; and, perhaps most important, local cultural, economic, social, and political realities and their relationship to the objectives of the stronger protagonist. To be sure, the United States could and should have prepared better for the aftermath of Saddam's ouster in Iraq and for the likely nature of the struggle in both Iraq and Afghanistan. But the larger lesson is that no amount of effort is likely to be able to overcome the political culture of a society, including such things as loyalty to sect or tribe over state, a winner-take-all (and loser-lose-all) approach to politics, historical balances between the capital and the periphery, the role of religion and the presence or absence of a secular divide, and the lure of traditional livelihoods and customs. "All politics is local" is the famous saying attributed to Tip O'Neill, the former speaker of the US House of Representatives; he might just as easily been referring to armed interventions.

Twenty-five years ago, Paul Kennedy outlined his thesis about imperial overstretch and the notion that great powers often ended up being anything but great as a result of impoverishing themselves in foreign folly.[10] A few years later, the Soviet Union would turn out to be Exhibit A; its demise came about as much because of decades of devoting too many resources to its military and a failed imperial venture in Afghanistan as it did from an inefficient economy and top-heavy politics. The question is whether Kennedy's idea now applies to the United States. Mostly it does not. The share of GDP that goes to all things related to national security is at sustainable and by historical standards not terribly high levels, nearly $800 billion out of $16 trillion, or about 5 percent. The immediate cost of seven years of war in Iraq is in the range of $1 trillion, a significant sum to be sure, but only some 4 percent of US federal spending during that same period. Cumulative costs for Afghanistan increase those numbers by only 50 percent.[11] And so, the two wars together amount to 15 percent of the debt accumulated since 2001. American imperial overstretch is, at most, a contributing cause of America's economic predicament. I point this out not to trivialize the significant costs of the Iraq and Afghanistan wars; rather, to underscore that the United States need not take risks with its security to rebuild economically.

America's lack of fiscal discipline has contributed far more to its loss of power and influence than have these wars. Lyndon Johnson was widely and rightly criticized for fighting an expensive war in Vietnam and markedly increasing domestic spending simultaneously. George W. Bush fought costly wars in Iraq and in Afghanistan, allowed discretionary domestic spending to increase at an annual rate of 6 percent, and cut taxes deeply.[12] The fiscal position of the United States declined in eight years from a surplus of just over $100 billion in 2001 (a year shared by the administrations of Bill Clinton and George W. Bush) to an estimated deficit of approximately $1.4 trillion in 2009 (a year shared by the Bush and Obama administrations.) As a result, the cumulative federal debt increased from just under $6 trillion in 2001 to $10 trillion over that same period. Although some of this spending and resultant jump in the deficit could be attributed to justified expenditures in the aftermath of 9/11 and the 2008 financial meltdown, much could not.

The many causes of the 2008 financial crisis are well known. At its core were inadequate regulation of the home mortgage market and the activities of large financial firms. As the economy went into recession, tax revenues dropped; at the same time, government spending was increased to jump-start the economy. Meanwhile, spending on entitlements also rose. The US budget deficit ballooned to between $1 and $1.5 trillion a year; by the end of 2012, the gross federal debt of the United States reached the size of its GDP. The United States had been set on an unsustainable path, one that would have to be corrected by its elected leaders through a mix of spending cuts and revenue increases or, failing that, that would leave the country vulnerable to forces outside its control.

The 2008 crisis, together with subsequent inability on the part of Congress and the executive branch to agree on a path forward to reduce the deficit and debt and restore traditional levels of economic growth, hurt the United States in another way: It diminished the appeal of the American economic and political model. The country's reputation for responsible global leadership took an additional hit when the United States took steps to accelerate its economic growth through "quantitative easing," steps that effectively increased the money supply, with little or no apparent concern for the rest of the world despite the fact that other governments held vast amounts of dollars (whose value would be reduced as the supply increased) and depended on the dollar for their international transactions.

China's Rise

We can debate whether America's unipolar moment ever existed, but there can be little doubt that bipolarity was the dominant feature of the international system for some four decades, from just after the end of World War II to the late 1980s and the crumbling of the Berlin Wall and, soon after, the collapse of the Soviet Union itself. The question for today is whether the world is again becoming bipolar, in this instance with China constituting the second pole.

China's rise is one of the defining features of this era. China has come a remarkably long way in a short time. Three and a half decades ago, at the end of the Cultural Revolution, China was home to some 900 million people with a GDP of under $200 billion. Today, population has increased by some 40 percent to 1.3 billion, but economic output has grown no less than 35 times, to $7 trillion!

Hundreds of millions of Chinese moved out of poverty and left rural areas for cities. GDP per capita rose from under $200 to more than $5,000. Five hundred million Chinese now use the Internet; cell phone usage is close to universal.[1] And despite significant controls and limits, China became a more open society than it was as well. During this period, it has mostly acted abroad with considerable caution, knowing it required external stability and financial support from the outside world to develop. Foreign policy was designed to serve domestic development, rather than the other way around.

One question: Going forward, can that high (double-digit) economic growth again be generated? If it could, it would ease important problems and pressures for China and its leaders. Above all, it would leave the bulk of the Chinese people relatively content with their system as it is. That said, high growth would be no panacea. For one thing, the gap between the distribution of economic power and political authority would continue to grow. The experience of other societies is that rising living standards and the emergence of a sizable middle class create pressures for greater pluralism. Economic inequality rankles. Accommodating such pressures would be difficult, to say the least, for a top-heavy authoritarian political system.

But far more likely for China is the opposite scenario, one in which growth slows considerably and stays well below double digits. Indeed, China's growth may have already fallen to as low as 5 or 6 percent; we cannot have great confidence in official statistics. Whatever the actual figure, simple realities of compounding make it difficult and ultimately impossible for China to keep growing at its high rate of recent decades. It is one thing to double GDP per capita over, say, seven years (a 10 percent annual growth rate) when it begins at $2,000 year. But assuming no increase in population it would take an increase of some $5,000 per person over the next seven years to sustain this rate of growth. Also, high rates of growth tend to be harder to sustain after much of the proverbial low-hanging fruit has been picked. Electricity can only be introduced once. Labor shortages, the result of an aging population and fewer Chinese moving to cities, have driven up the costs of manufacturing, one reason that other producers of relatively inexpensive goods are now providing stiff competition to China. In addition, years of low economic growth in Europe, Japan, and to a lesser extent the United States (and the prospect of additional such years to come) have limited these areas' ability to absorb Chinese goods. There is also increasing resistance around the world to China's policy of keeping its currency at artificially low levels to reduce the cost of its exports to consumers in Europe and the United States.

All this creates profound pressures for China's leaders. Much of the legitimacy of its ruling elite stems from their ability to produce robust economic performance. For more than three decades, China has depended on double-digit economic growth, largely generated by ever-increasing exports, to maintain high levels of employment, raise living standards, and thereby assure social tranquility. In many ways, materialism came to replace socialism as the dominant "ism" of contemporary China.

This era—one launched by Deng Xiaoping in the aftermath of the Cultural Revolution and that has dominated that country for more than three decades—is now ending. At the same time, domestic pressures, including the need to raise hundreds of millions more Chinese out of poverty, growing resentment over income and wealth inequality, widespread desire for a higher standard of living, and the demand to provide more health and retirement benefits, are also pushing China's leaders to find something to complement export-led growth. The result is that China is in the early days of a profound transition, one in which economic growth will increasingly have to stem from increased domestic and consumer-driven demand rather than from exports and state spending on large infrastructure projects. Like all transitions, this sort of rebalancing is easier to call for than to bring about.

Finding the proverbial Goldilocks course—say, growth that averages maybe 7 to 8 percent a year through, among other things, the gradual substitution of domestic consumption for lost exports—will be difficult. China is constrained by a deteriorating environment (when I was last in Beijing, I could see only a few hundred meters and it was painful to breathe), a large and aging population where fewer workers will have to support a growing number of retirees, large social needs, and a top-heavy political system that is far less dynamic than its economy. Creating a country that could innovate on a large scale would require introducing educational and social reforms that would only feed the desire for additional political change, something the leadership resists. If that same political system cannot continue to deliver improved living standards for 500 million people who are still poor by any measure, it will eventually come under direct challenge, although just how quickly is unclear. Already, there are 100,000 political protests of some scale per year in China over grievances ranging from land confiscation and corruption to unemployment and environmental problems.[2]

The question arises as to how the Communist Party will react as growth slows. There are in principle three paths: limited reform; some mixture of regression and repression; and appeal to nationalism. Introducing economic and political reform would be the most desirable and in the long run beneficial, but it could lead to calls for fundamental change, including the end to the Communist Party's dominant role. Reform could also create considerable social disorder throughout the country, something feared by many Chinese to a degree rarely appreciated by outsiders. For these and other reasons, China's rulers are unlikely to embrace reform in a wholesale or rapid fashion; instead, their approach to it will probably be one of selectivity and caution.

Repression is not a sustainable proposition in the long run; nor is a return to Maoist orthodoxy. The latter cannot produce the rates of needed economic growth. But a degree of repression on top of what already exists is a real possibility if, as seems likely, criticism and protests grow amid economic slowdown. And calls for a return to the Maoist tradition are sure to be heard if disorder begins to mount and corruption continues at current levels.

Another possibility would be for China's rulers to wrap themselves in the flag and further embrace nationalism. For many years, Chinese officials and academics articulated a concept of its peaceful rise so as not to alienate its neighbors.[3] But China's heavy-handed approach toward nearby countries (in particular Japan, the Philippines, and Vietnam) over competing claims to territorial seas and islands is cause for concern. The obvious danger is that this behavior is a harbinger of a more assertive or even aggressive China, a development that would complicate, if not end, prospects for significant collaboration on regional and global challenges and raise the prospect of a twenty-first-century version of a cold war. Until now, China's foreign policy has mostly taken a backseat to its economic development. Claims on Taiwan, just to name one prominent example, were never pressed militarily. China has opted for stability and commercial ties over most else. But this restraint may not last. The irony is inescapable: Political leaders in the United States and Asia are busy debating how best to meet what they perceive as the threat from China; political leaders in China are debating how best to meet the many threats they perceive to China, including its encirclement by countries determined to block its rise and internal threats to its stability and even unity.

China's three possible paths are by no means mutually exclusive; to the contrary, we are likely to see a mix of selective reform, heightened state control, and bouts of nationalism. As is already evident, a wealthier China will become a stronger China, and such a China will want to exert influence commensurate with its increased strength. China is building up and modernizing its military. The real question is whether it will use this strength to bolster the international order and, among other things, to help bridge the gap that has grown between various global challenges and existing arrangements as well as do more to help resolve regional conflicts.

China's behavior toward North Korea is less than fully reassuring. The Korean Peninsula remains divided, one of the last monuments of the Cold War. This situation exists in no small part because China subsidizes North Korea despite the risks posed to its own interests by its often irresponsible and unpredictable partner. The reason is partly strategic, in that China would view a unified peninsula with its capital in Seoul and in the American strategic orbit as constituting a major strategic setback. It is worth keeping in mind that China intervened in the Korean War precisely to prevent the unification of the entire country under the aegis of the United Nations, then dominated by the United States. There are also political ties between Chinese leaders and their North Korean counterparts, and some concerns in China that a crisis involving the North could trigger large flows of refugees into China. The point is not that Chinese troops would necessarily intervene again if war erupted; rather, that China is not ready to put aside relatively narrow national concerns to pursue a foreign policy that would enhance regional and global order.

China's pattern of investing in and buying up energy and mineral resources around the world is also cause for concern. At the end of the day, though, China cannot buy its way to guaranteeing access to sufficient energy and mineral resources it will need to sustain its long-term growth; it must soon face the choice of joining the United States and others to promote the stability of energy-producing countries and the security of transit routes or face the consequences of supply shortages and price increases. China is too big an actor with the need to import and export on too large a scale to be able to wall itself off from the realities of globalization.

That said, there is as yet little evidence that China is prepared to take on a regional or global role that transcends narrowly defined national interests. Chinese officials often protest that their country is still developing and ought not to be expected to put international responsibilities before national ones. While on one level this stance is understandable, it is also self-serving and possibly not even that, as China (which, for example, imports more than one-third the oil it consumes from the Middle East and is highly vulnerable to the effects of climate change) has a large and growing stake in regional stability and global cooperation.

It is helpful, too, to maintain perspective. China may have the world's second-largest economy, and in several decades may well have the world's largest, overtaking even the United States, but per capita output is at most only a fifth that of the most developed countries. Hundreds of millions of Chinese remain below the poverty line. China has reason to avoid acting recklessly: Not only could it devalue its own considerable dollar holdings if it acted in ways that hurt the US economy and weakened the dollar, but, perhaps more important, China still needs decades' more external stability if it is to be able to do all it wants to develop internally. Although China is building up militarily, its overall military spending is only a fraction that of the United States, and what China deploys is far behind US equipment in quality. The issue should not be China's rise, which is inevitable even if many observers underestimate the looming hurdles, but what the character shall be, at home and abroad, of a more powerful China.[4]

A Post-European World

We are living in a post-European world. Indeed, we are in the early stages of what might be termed the post-European era of international relations. Partly this is an ironic result of Europe's success. The continent that was the locale of so much turmoil (including two world wars and a cold war) during the past century is largely whole, free, and calm. France, Germany, and Great Britain, three of the principal protagonists of twentieth-century history, are fully and seemingly permanently reconciled. Europe is, by a long shot, the most integrated of regions, the part of the world where area-wide institutions and rules play the most significant part in the lives of the area's countries and their citizens. The biggest problems in contemporary Europe tend to be about budgets, not bombs, and financing welfare, not war.

In some ways, the contrast between Europe and Asia could hardly be more dramatic. Asia will be, before long, the center of gravity of the world economy; the historic question is whether its dynamism can be managed peacefully. Asian regional mechanisms, especially in the political and security realms, are comparatively thin. The United States, China, Japan,

India, Vietnam, Russia, the two Koreas, Indonesia, Australia, the Philippines, and others eye one another warily. Much remains unresolved, from territorial claims to historical grievances. Competition and friction are unavoidable; conflict is a possibility that cannot be ruled out. The twenty-first century is far more likely to kick up dust in the Asia-Pacific region than it is in Europe.

But another truth about Europe is less positive. Despite a collective GDP slightly larger than that of the United States and a population of over 500 million, Europe punches far below its weight in the world as a result of its parochialism, its pronounced antimilitary culture, and the unresolved tensions between the pull of nationalism and the commitment to building a collective union. For these and related reasons, Europe, the principal strategic and economic partner of the United States in the world for more than half a century, is likely to be less significant in the half-century ahead.

Take defense. The problem is not the number of European troops; there are nearly two million. Nor is it so much what Europeans spend on defense: some $250 billion a year, roughly half of US defense spending. Rather, it is how those troops are organized and how that money is spent. The whole is far less than the sum of its parts, in part because decisions are made nationally. Much of the discussion about a common foreign and defense policy never translates into action. Precious little has been done to promote specialization or coordination. National politics and economics dictate expenditures: There is much replication of what is not relevant and little is invested in what is truly needed. Missing in particular are many of the assets needed to project military force across distances, to areas more likely than continental Europe to be the battlefields of the future.[1]

There is also a political and cultural problem. Even where a willingness to intervene with military force exists, such as in Libya or Afghanistan, there are significant constraints. Some governments refuse to participate in combat operations. European political culture has evolved in ways that make it more difficult to field modern militaries prepared to bear the cost in blood and treasure; then secretary of defense Robert Gates described what has happened as "the demilitarization of Europe— where large swaths of the general public and political class are averse to military force and the risks that go with it." All this inevitably limits NATO's future role, as NATO mostly makes sense as an expeditionary force in an often unstable world, not as a standing army on a mostly stable continent. Indeed, Gates went on to warn that NATO faced "the very real possibility of collective military irrelevance."[2]

Europe's loss of centrality goes beyond the defense sphere to reflect financial, economic, political, and demographic realities. The European project, which in its most ambitious form dreamed of a single market and a single continental political entity, is foundering. Popular rejections of the 2007 Lisbon Treaty (which aimed to strengthen European institutions at the expense of national ones), as well as the treaty to establish a new constitution that preceded it, demonstrate that the notion of a truly united Europe has become more the cause of the elite, one that no longer captures the imagination of a majority of the continent's residents. Lackluster leadership of European organizations is both a cause and a result of this loss of momentum. Behind this drift is the stark reality that Europeans have never quite committed to Europe—a "United States of Europe"—in large part because of the continued pull of nationalism; the region remains much closer to a "United Europe of States." This is especially true for the younger generation, which tends not to see the EU as an essential solution to such historical challenges as German nationalism or a Russian threat.[3] If Europeans were serious about being a unified power, they would trade the British and French United Nations Security Council seats for a European one. This is not about to happen.

The decision taken two decades ago to create a monetary union without a fiscal counterpart was a structural error. Something had to give, and it did in the wake of the 2008 financial crisis and recession begun in the United States. Greece has become something of a poster child for what ails Europe, but the culprit just as easily could have been (and, with time, may well turn out to be) Spain, Portugal, Italy, or even France. The thread running through these mostly southern European countries and the challenges they face is a mix of their own profligacy—above all, extensive, costly social programs built on modest economic foundations, debt, or both—and a weak EU leadership that permitted them to live beyond their means and violate the terms under which the euro was established. Making the crisis both more severe and prolonged alike were the relatively timid responses from European institutions and governments. (The comparison with the number and scale of measures introduced in 2008–2009 by the US government, including economic stimulus, quantitative easing, corporate bailouts, and the Troubled Asset Relief Program [TARP], is both marked and instructive.) Europe's politics have never caught up with its finances.

But the European economic challenge is far larger than the Eurozone. The financial crisis hopefully will be managed (not to be equated with solved) by a mixture of bottom-up improvements that rein in spending and increase tax collection in select European countries and, more likely, through top-down measures that will increase the liquidity of banks and governments' access to capital. But that is very different than addressing the underlying economic condition, one that reflects structural problems and weaknesses. Europe faces a future of prolonged low growth as a result of many factors: overly generous entitlements including early retirement coupled with generous pensions, high taxation, low labor mobility, extensive regulation, broad resistance to immigration, a paucity of venture capital, and legal regimes that discourage risk-taking by making recovery from failure and bankruptcy extremely difficult.[4] Even taking into account such exceptions as Germany, Europe's overall recovery is likely to be modest at best in both absolute and relative terms.

Time and demographics will not improve the situation. Europe's population has leveled off at about 500 million and is rapidly aging. By midcentury, the ratio of retirees to those of working age is projected to double.[5] Fewer will be of military age; a smaller number will be working to support the many that are retired. Europe, representing one-fourth of the world's economic output, slightly more than the United States, is now the world's largest economy, but it won't be for long. It faces a future that is more likely to resemble Japan's than China's; for economic and political reasons alike, Europe's position as a major power in the twenty-first-century world looks to be all but over.

The Wannabe
Major Powers

At least in principle, it could be argued that this is a multipolar world; that is, one dominated by a few. The principal powers—the United States, China, Japan, Europe, India, and Russia—contain over half the world's people. They also account for nearly three-fourths of global GDP and an even higher percentage of what the world spends on defense.

But as already noted, the trends do not favor the emergence of traditional multipolarity. One reason is the existence of another fifteen or twenty countries with real capacity. The fact that the G-20 (which in reality often comes closer to the G-25) has largely replaced the G-8 is instructive here. And then there is the increasing number and significance of organizations and forces other than states.

A second reality is that the so-called great powers are not all that great. China has already been discussed, as has Europe. Both have significant vulnerabilities and weaknesses along with their strengths. And the United States is, for all of its capacity and promise, both underperforming and overreaching.

But what about Japan, until recently the world's second-largest economy, and now its third? Its wealth per person is nine times higher than that of China. Japan also possesses one of the world's most capable militaries, spending some $50 billion annually on defense. It is a stable society with modern infrastructure.

Japan, however, is unlikely to be a major factor in the world any time soon beyond the economic realm. The population is slightly above 100 million, less than a tenth of China's, just over a third of America's. It is saddled with a large debt—approximately 200 percent of GDP.[1] A lack of immigration denies Japan not just an opportunity to increase its population and lower its average age, but to obtain new ideas and talent. Japan is heavily dependent on imports of raw materials and access to markets for its exports. It is limited by an aging society, political parties that are more personal fiefdoms than dynamic organizations, and the burden of its history that makes most of its neighbors wary of any sign of its reemergence as a regional political and military power. Japan's constitution, a result of World War II, still limits the role of the Japanese armed forces to self-defense; formally amending it so that Japan could become a more "normal" country, one able to deploy and employ a modern, capable military force like other countries, would trigger intense internal and regional resistance alike. Like Europe's, Japan's impact in the world will be less than it could or would be, were its domestic politics different.[2]

Then there is India. India will pass China as the world's most populous country in a matter of decades. India is arguably more resilient than China; its democracy, now more than sixty years old, gives it a flexibility that China's more brittle system does not. India's economy has also fared quite well, growing at an average rate of 6 percent a year since 1980. India's GDP is now approaching $2 trillion; its position in the world of information technology is secure. India's military is modernizing across the board.

But India is not without significant constraints; there is a second India. Its enormous population, like China's, is as much burden as resource. Hundreds of millions of Indians live in poverty. A good deal of education remains substandard. Corruption is widespread. Economic growth is further limited by inadequate transportation and electricity-related infrastructure, while quality of life is constrained not just by these shortcomings but from severe problems in the realms of water, housing, and sewage. The population is divided by language and ethnicity; caste bias is still prevalent, limiting social mobility. Unwieldy coalitions at the national level, together with overlapping powers at the federal and state levels, make for sclerotic government that is often hostage to the agendas of regional or marginal parties far out of the political mainstream.[3]

India is also constrained by geography. It is bordered by both China and Pakistan. India and China are wary of each other, but their policies are mostly kept in check despite a still-unsettled border and memories of a war fought a half-century ago. Nonetheless, their proximity is a consideration, one that now fuels India's nuclear and missile programs and influences India's conventional force levels and deployments.

Pakistan is a far more problematic neighbor for India, not because it is stronger, but because so many Pakistanis view India as an existential threat. Pakistan has defined itself for much of its history in opposition to India; the differences thus go beyond contested territory in Kashmir, although that is surely part of the explanation. There is a history of conflict and barely averted conflict. The risk for India is not just terrorism emanating from Pakistan, but the danger that renewed conventional military conflict could escalate into nuclear war. Despite the lack of appeal of Pakistan's often violent and dysfunctional model, there is as well the potential for incitement of some of the estimated 175 million Indian Muslims, a possibility that could come to pose challenges to India's unity and stability. The Indo-Pakistani relationship is mostly undeveloped; the two countries have less commercial, diplomatic, and cultural interaction than did the United States and the Soviet Union at the height of the Cold War.[4]

It is in India's own interest to meet Pakistan more than half-way in an attempt to settle or at least reduce their outstanding differences. But Indians are disinclined to do this—they are too bitter and suspicious after decades of confrontation—and Pakistan's military leadership (which has a dominant political role) is unlikely to accept Indian offers of compromise that fall short of the former's maximum demands. India, therefore, is unlikely to free itself from the costs and risks central to its relationship with Pakistan—and for this reason (among others, including the lack of much that would qualify as serious thought and debate about its international role) India is unlikely to soon realize its potential in the region or the world.

Russia is another member of the club of would-be great powers. Even after the breakup of the Soviet Union, Russia remains the world's largest country in the territorial sense. It enjoys great natural resources, including oil and gas. It has the only nuclear arsenal in the same league as that of the United States. It is one of the five veto-wielding, permanent members of the United Nations Security Council.

But Russia has been and will continue to be held back. It is hobbled by corruption and a top-heavy political system that functions more like an oligarchy than a democracy; the possibility even exists for large-scale popular protest—a "Moscow

Spring," so to speak—that would challenge the legitimacy and durability of the regime. Russia has a mostly one-dimensional economy, one more influenced by government than markets, that is heavily dependent on oil, gas, and minerals. The population is down to 142 million and, until recently, was declining by several hundred thousand a year, the result of alcoholism, disease, crime, and a poor public health system.[5] Large tracts of the country are lightly populated. Ethnic divisions and separatist inclinations are pronounced. The military is relatively weak and lagging in the way of modern arms, support systems, and training. The last twenty years have not been good in many ways for Russians; they have lost half their country and considerable influence, and seen NATO enlarge up to their borders. President Putin has exploited this sense of humiliation and resentment, but has done little to set Russia on a path that would allow it to be a great power in fact as well as name.[6]

As the title of this section suggests, the countries conventionally listed as great powers are in fact something less than that. There is a positive side to this from the American vantage point, as it strongly suggests a lack of direct challenge. But there is also a negative, as countries that are less than great and preoccupied with domestic or local challenges make for poor partners. This is a serious problem, given the limits on US capacities and the reality that this is a world of multiple challenges that often require a collective response.

The Global Gap

Beyond their individual weaknesses and vulnerabilities, the major powers share a common predicament: their inability to agree on how the world is to be organized and operated. The result is a gap between what exists and what is needed in the way of global rules and arrangements to enable globalization's positive effects and inhibit its negative ones. Accounting for this "global gap" is the absence of consensus as to the rules necessary for governing international relations and to the penalties for breaking them.

There are of course any number of international organizations, from the United Nations and the International Monetary Fund to the World Health Organization and the World Trade Organization. But they all fall short of what is needed. Part of the problem is that many of these institutions were designed at and for a different time. Many originated during or soon after World War II, when the world was dominated by the Allies, which included the United States, Great Britain, the Soviet Union, and France. There was no (or at most a severely limited) role for Axis countries such as Germany and Japan, and little provision for colonial areas that would soon emerge as states.

In the case of climate change, there is near-universal acceptance among the world's governments of the scientific evidence that burning fossil fuels is causing measurable change in the earth's climate, something that in turn will affect not just average temperatures but agricultural output, species survival, insect and disease prevalence, severity and frequency of tornadoes and hurricanes, and flooding in coastal areas. But taking the kinds of steps that would have a meaningful effect on carbon emissions has proven impossible, given that any such pact would constrain economic activity (anathema to developed countries suffering from low or no economic growth) and slow the extension of access to energy and electricity to literally hundreds of millions of people in developing countries, something unacceptable to China and India, which do not accept that their middle classes should be denied the benefits their Western counterparts have experienced. The result is that the world will face a future in which significant climate change is a reality—already, the temperature of both the oceans and the atmosphere is substantially higher, as are sea levels—and where, as a result, the policy debate will come to focus less on mitigation and more on how best to adapt to altered conditions or even geoengineering, a controversial approach bordering on science fiction with the potential to reverse the warming through such steps as adding particles to the atmosphere that would filter out some sunlight.[1]

Stopping the spread of nuclear weapons would seem to be a significantly more promising issue, as consensus and collaboration alike can be identified. The Nonproliferation Treaty (NPT), which came into force in 1970 and is now signed by 189 countries, limits the right to possess nuclear weapons to the five permanent members of the Security Council, making clear as well that this right is temporary, as these countries are expected to reduce and ultimately eliminate their arsenals. Also, several supplementary arrangements are in place among potential suppliers of critical relevant technologies to deny these components or technologies to would-be proliferators.

But agreement is thinner than it first appears. The Nonproliferation Treaty allows countries the right to develop nuclear energy for purposes such as electricity generation, a loophole that allows governments the ability to put into place most of what is necessary to produce the critical fuel for a nuclear weapon. The associated inspection regime created in 1957 under the International Atomic Energy Agency (IAEA) to make sure that nothing untoward is going on is in fact a gentlemen's club; inspectors only have the right to inspect facilities that are made known to them by the government in question. Governments (such as Iran's) can and do carry out illegal nuclear activities in secret sites that international inspectors either do not know about or, even if they do, cannot gain entry to. The so-called Additional Protocol, created just over a decade ago, provides for a more assertive inspections regime to ensure that activities inconsistent with the treaty's purpose are less likely to take place, but adherence to this, too, is voluntary. Nor is there international agreement on a comprehensive ban of all nuclear tests, something that would further inhibit weapons development.

At least as important, there is no agreement among the major powers as to what to do when a country refuses to sign the NPT—Israel, India, and Pakistan all come to mind—or violates it, as North Korea and Iran have done. Israel, India, Pakistan, and North Korea paid little price for developing nuclear weapons. In each case, one or more major power patrons had reason to look the other way when the country in question moved toward and finally across the nuclear weapons threshold. Iran, the most recent test for the global nonproliferation regime, has paid a considerable price for its nuclear-related activities, but the record suggests that shared opposition in principle to a country's gaining nuclear weapons does not translate into common policies; many of the sanctions aimed at Iran are subscribed to only by a subset of governments.

Closely related to a lack of agreement on many facets of what to do to frustrate nuclear proliferation is the clear disagreement over the legality and legitimacy of undertaking preventive military action to stop it. There is considerable legal and diplomatic underpinning for a country's right to intervene militarily to thwart an imminent threat from another state or entity. Such acts of preemption are seen as synonymous with the notion of "anticipatory self-defense." What matters again is that the threat of attack is both incontrovertible and imminent: a destructive capacity not only completed but being readied for actual use. If these criteria are met, then a state has the right to preempt, or strike, before it is struck.[2]

This is something fundamentally different from preventive action: intervention against a threat that is gathering but not yet fully developed, much less being readied for immediate use. Preventive action was contemplated by the Soviet Union against China in the late 1960s and discouraged by the United States, which saw potential leverage against the USSR in the rise of a China that was competitive with it. Israel carried out preventive attacks against nuclear-related facilities in Iraq in 1981 and Syria in 2007. In 2003, the United States carried out what it incorrectly described as a preemptive war but was in fact a preventive war against Iraq. To the extent Iraq constituted a threat in the realm of weapons of mass destruction, it was gathering; their use was not imminent. In the event, it was later learned that the threat was not even gathering.

This has all become much more than an arcane academic matter, given the Iranian nuclear program and concerns about the destabilizing consequences of Iran's approaching or reaching nuclear weapons status. Israel and the United States are both contemplating preventive military action. The question is what the international reaction would be if either or both were to go ahead. There is also the precedential dimension of acting, as a world of repeated preventive strikes by one state against another for reasons including, but not necessarily limited to, thwarting nuclear spread, could well become extraordinarily dangerous and messy. Ideally, there would be agreement both on the conditions that would constitute a legitimate preventive strike and the procedure for gaining international legal and diplomatic support for undertaking one. Such a globally accepted norm could also act as a deterrent to a country going down the proliferation path; be that as it may, such agreement is a long ways off.

More international cooperation exists in the realm of economics than in any other, mostly because such cooperation is so patently in the interests of individual countries. This includes not just trade but also monetary policy, investment, development, and financial regulation. This last area has perhaps seen the greatest degree of progress in recent years, spurred in large part by the 2008 crisis and its aftermath. The G-20 governments, meeting in Seoul in late 2010, approved new guidelines to be phased in gradually for, among other things, the amount of capital banks need to keep on hand. Such commitments form part of a larger set of arrangements that are broadly observed, such as those that set standards for accounting. The decision to accept such rules must be taken by individual governments, but there is incentive to do so lest they discourage investment and other forms of business activity in and with their country.[3]

Trade, however, is the area of the highest degree of international integration. Modern arrangements go back to the immediate post–World War II years, when some two dozen countries established the General Agreement on Tariffs and Trade (GATT), a forum designed to lower tariff and other trade barriers widely viewed to have contributed to the Great Depression and the run-up to World War II. In 1995, the GATT was replaced by the World Trade Organization (WTO). The GATT and WTO have made real progress over these decades toward reducing and eliminating tariff barriers that impede trade; the WTO has also established a dispute-resolution mechanism that all 157 of its members subscribe to.

Progress on expanding trade has slowed, however, in recent years. This is another case of multilateralism's having become too unwieldy. The most recent round of global trade talks, started up in Doha in 2001, has failed to produce consensus between developed and developing countries on the treatment of agricultural goods, the elimination of trade-distorting subsidies, and some aspects of trade in manufacturing. Another problem is that the WTO has no ability to deal with currency manipulation (a charge often leveled against China), a practice that distorts trade by making the goods of some countries artificially inexpensive. Again, this is an arena in which principles come into direct conflict with domestic political and economic realities. Bilateral and regional trade pacts are, at best, an incomplete substitute for global arrangements as by definition they fail to address certain issues (such as farm subsidies) and many markets. The price of this inability to progress on a broad front is both economic—estimates are that the United States could, with substantial trade liberalization, increase its GDP by as much as $500 billion a year—and political, as trade constitutes a potential barrier to conflict between and among countries that have a strong disincentive not to interrupt relations working to their mutual benefit.[4] Global trade negotiations, for decades the leading edge of multilateralism, have hit a wall.

Foreign investment is less regulated internationally than trade. Just about every government wants to attract foreign investment as it can fuel development of natural resources, manufacturing, and/or infrastructure development. It is especially appealing to developing economies (which hope it involves not just funding but technology transfer) and cash-strapped developed countries. At the same time, governments want to wall off areas of not just narrow security significance but also economic advantage. Ought there, then, to be some sort of WIO—World Investment Organization—that would establish principles guiding foreign investment along with a dispute resolution mechanism for those inevitable occasions when there were clashes? Efforts to create such a framework—a multilateral agreement on investment—came to naught in the 1990s, largely because a disparate collection of left-leaning advocacy groups generated considerable opposition and controversy that few countries were prepared to take on.[5] Today, nearly two decades later, there is little interest in resuming such negotiations, in part because governments fear they would see their ability to limit investment (be it for reasons of commercial competitiveness or security) curtailed. What we are seeing instead is the proliferation of bilateral investment treaties. Literally thousands exist, but with the lack of consistency and inclusion, global investment flows are not as large as they could be while the friction generated by disputes relating to denied opportunities for investment is greater than it should be.

Shortcomings exist in other aspects of the global economic machinery. The International Monetary Fund (IMF) can refuse to loan money to a government in need unless certain terms are met, something that can provide useful leverage in promoting needed reform when it comes to pressuring countries that seek to borrow. The IMF can also assess the adequacy of individual country policies and regulatory frameworks as well as estimate their growth prospects, though it cannot require them to reform their ways if they don't wish to borrow directly from it. In addition, the decision-making of the IMF, like many institutions, has not kept up with shifts in the global distribution of wealth; China, along with many of the oil-rich countries, is underrepresented, although owing to some recent changes, the situation is better than it was.[6]

If economics highlights a persistent gap between global machinery and long-standing challenges, cyberspace reflects the gap between global rules and emerging issues. In some ways it is reminiscent of nuclear arms control back in the 1950s, when the technology outpaced the conceptual thinking. It took decades to catch up, and even now there is still something of a gap, given the politics of national security. When it comes to cyberspace, there is little in the way of machinery. The International Telecommunications Union (ITU) has nominal jurisdiction of this domain, but so far at least there has been discussion with little agreement.

Behind this lack of legal and political frameworks is the reality that there is, as yet, no consensus on what is to be protected versus restricted or banned or regulated. The United States, in part because of its massive reliance on information technology for everything from financial operations to defense, is most concerned about cyber security and the protection of networks and infrastructure. Some now speak of cyberspace as a fifth national security domain, alongside ground, air, sea, and space. There is also a strong American preference for an interconnected world in which information and ideas flow freely. Thus, it comes as no surprise that US policy is to promote a "secure, open, reliable, and globally connected" IT architecture in which access to the Internet is a human right and in which individual privacy is a major consideration.[7]

Others, and in particular authoritarian governments, are more concerned about information security—the ability to control what is available on the Internet and social media. Their concern is less about protecting physical and economic infrastructure than about maintaining political and social stability. More widespread international concerns include whether and how to filter content to prevent the Internet from being used for pornography, hate speech, or terrorist training and recruiting. The disagreement between the United States, which favors free speech even when it causes offense (a crude Internet video produced in the United States was found to be highly offensive by most Muslims in September 2012) and many governments in the Arab and Muslim worlds, is telling. Nor is there anything approaching agreement among governments on what are the rights as well as obligations of states, what constitutes an aggressive act, or when acts of cyber aggression (such as those employed against Iran's nuclear program) might be permitted. Further complicating efforts in the cyber arena is the prevalence of nonstate actors. Just to be clear: The intention here is not to argue that the goal should be agreement for agreement's sake, as it should not—a bad consensus is worse than none it all—rather, to highlight how in this area, too, there is little in the way of actual global accord.[8]

Health is yet another realm where global arrangements fall short of what is required. The World Health Organization (WHO), created in 1948 to fight disease and promote health, has a limited mandate that leaves it ill-prepared to fulfill its mission in the modern world. Calls for increased international cooperation on matters of health have grown of late, more than anything the result of concerns triggered by the SARS outbreak of 2003 and fears about pandemic influenza. The concerns are well founded, as in a global world, what begins in the most remote region of one country can quickly spread around the world via modern travel. Unfortunately, few clear rules exist for what governments need to do to contribute to global efforts to contain any outbreak of infectious disease.

The 2005 International Health Regulations, endorsed by almost all the world's governments, were designed to help fill this gap.[9] Governments agreed on a common strategy to detect disease outbreaks and notify the WHO when they occurred. However, dozens of countries have fallen behind on establishing such a capacity; in many cases, they lack the technical means as well as the financial wherewithal. There is even less agreement on non communicable diseases (NCDs), including cancer, heart and lung diseases, and diabetes, which often stem from tobacco and alcohol use, inactivity, and diet. A 2011 UN summit accomplished little.[10] So while there has been some progress, even in a relatively apolitical area such as combating disease, the world is far from being the community it needs to be.

One last area where the appearance of international progress does not quite comport with the reality involves humanitarian intervention. The issue gained considerable prominence in the initial post–Cold War decade as a result of actions taken (Somalia, Bosnia, and Kosovo) and not taken (Rwanda, Congo, Sudan). Failure to act when international intervention might have saved large numbers of innocent lives generated the idea of sovereignty as responsibility, namely, that sovereignty entails obligations as well as rights, and when governments fail to meet these obligations, either out of choice or a lack of capacity, they forfeit some of their rights.[11]

Most of us can agree that governments that attack their own people on a large scale, or which allow such attacks to be carried out by one group of citizens against another, open themselves up to humanitarian intervention by outsiders. This notion was enshrined in 2005 by the United Nations, which stated that in such situations the international community took on the "Responsibility to Protect," or R2P.[12]

But there has been more than a little "buyer's remorse" ever since. The difference here between international reactions to aggression between states and to aggression within them is both striking and telling. The world came together to repudiate and, in the end, reverse Saddam Hussein's invasion and occupation of Kuwait in 1990–1991. What was at issue then was sovereignty and the ability to use military force to overwhelm it. This was almost universally rejected, just as Kuwait's right of self-defense was almost universally embraced. These concepts lie at the heart of the modern international system of independent states that can be traced back to the mid-seventeenth century. Here at least there is genuine community around the world; self-interest has its virtues.

Despite the existence of R2P, no such consensus exists on the right of the international community to intervene in internal situations. Many governments are concerned that this new concept can raise expectations that they will act—something that could prove costly in lives, military expenditures, and, depending on the circumstances, commercial and other national interests. Even more, a number of governments are worried that R2P could be turned on them, that their sovereignty could be "violated" by the international community under circumstances in which they might believe their own actions to be totally warranted or when they judge the situation does not justify R2P. Russian and Chinese reticence in pressuring governments that deserve censure and sanction is largely derived from such concerns; such reticence was reinforced when the 2012 humanitarian intervention in Libya evolved into something much closer to imposed regime change.

These differences came to a head in 2012 with Syria. The United States, much of Europe, and many of the Sunni Arab countries saw the Syrian government's large-scale and violent attacks on its own people as warranting a response, including severe sanctions and assistance to the opposition, though there was little enthusiasm for undertaking what promised to be a difficult armed intervention. For their part, China and Russia, as well as Iran, opposed such international pressure and actions for reasons that reflected their regional aims as well as their general concerns about R2P. Instead, they worked to bolster the regime of Bashar al-Assad through economic and military support. The split in the international community helped the regime hang on. Kofi Annan, for a year the UN special envoy to the crisis in Syria, asked upon resigning, "Is ours an international community that will act in defence of the most vulnerable of our world and make the necessary sacrifices to help?"[13] For now, at least, the answer is no. As a result, the phrase "international community" is in this realm, as in others, more aspiration than reality; the gap between global challenges and effective international arrangements is all too real.

None of this is meant as a call for despair or to make the case for unilateralism. But multilateralism will necessarily need to become more varied. On occasion it will take what might be described as the classic form: formal and universal, as represented by the United Nations. But this will be the exception, given how difficult it will be to gain consensus among the 193 countries of the General Assembly or even among all of the major powers. We are more likely to see narrower pacts; in the trade sphere, for example, there will be a growing number of regional and bilateral alternatives to a new global accord. Or in the climate realm, if, as seems virtually certain, a global carbon tax or global permit system remains impossible to negotiate, one can imagine "mini-agreements" that would set minimum common standards for vehicle fuel efficiency or slow the deforestation that accounts for as much as one-fifth of the problem. More broadly, we can anticipate seeing more regional undertakings, limited groupings determined by capacity (the G-20), relevance (the six-party mechanism designed to deal with North Korea), outlook (the Proliferation Security Initiative), coalitions of the willing, or simply agreements between countries to do their best to steer their domestic policy in a specified area in a specified direction. Such "informalism" has been seen in the financial realm in the aftermath of the crisis of 2008. All of these alternatives to the "classic" multilateralism place a premium on intellectual creativity and diplomatic skill.

Shortfalls in global arrangements can be offset at the regional level, but only up to a point. Regional organizations tend to be most significant in the economic realm; this is certainly the case in Europe and Asia. But they tend to fall short in the diplomatic and security realms, usually because consensus is absent and capacity is lacking. Regional bodies in the Middle East, South Asia, Latin America, and Africa have proven mostly ineffectual. The "regional gap" is most significant in Asia, the locale of many of the world's most powerful and dynamic countries. China, Japan, South Korea, and Russia have yet to do away with disagreements dating back to the Second World War. The Korean peninsula remains divided, a vestige of the Cold War, while the region's most populous countries, China and India, still struggle with border disagreements and a more basic competition based on mutual suspicion. China and several of its neighbors have staked out competing claims to the South China Sea, and China and Japan squared off in the fall of 2012 over the fate of some small, uninhabited islands— the Senkakus in Japan, the Diaoyus in China—that the two countries could not even agree what to call. The obvious danger is that all this competition and dynamism spills over, leading to a twenty-first-century Asia that resembles nothing so much as early twentieth-century Europe.

What is obvious is that the gap is large between what the world requires to be safe and prosperous and what exists, reflecting a lack of intellectual creativity, institutional capacity, and political consensus. The existence of such a global gap increases the odds that the balance between forces promoting order and disorder in the world could tip toward the latter, resulting in military conflicts, the spread and ultimately use of nuclear weapons, terrorism on a grand scale, catastrophic climate change, obstacles to trade and financial and investment flows, rampant cyber and other forms of crime, and pandemics, in turn providing great potential for a substantial loss in safety, prosperity, and freedom. Narrowing the gap will be difficult; it will not simply happen. Again, the United States has more capacity and experience of leading collective efforts to deal with common challenges than has anyone else. The question going forward is not simply whether the United States will find partners, but whether it will be able and willing to play its traditional role.

Reason for Optimism

The most important and overlooked feature of the contemporary world is that great power conflict is highly unlikely for the foreseeable future. Great power suspicion and competition and rivalry have not disappeared and will not, but neither are they likely to spill over into conflict, much less all-out war. This is worth emphasizing because more than anything else, it distinguishes the first half of this century from virtually all of the century that preceded it. The twentieth century was defined by two world wars and a cold war that mercifully stayed that way; the twenty-first century is starting out and promises to remain for some time something qualitatively different.

This difference brings with it important benefits. The first and most obvious is what is being avoided: namely, some of the costs of preparing for great power war and all of the human, economic, and military costs of fighting one. This is not to suggest, as quite a few observers have done, that war between countries (as opposed to within, which is all too common) is largely or entirely thing of the past because of interdependence, economic pressures, the destructiveness of modern weapons, and widespread changes in thinking.[1] Alas, wars between states are all too imaginable, whether out of design, recklessness, or miscalculation. But the possibility of war in the foreseeable future does not seem to include anything on the scale of the twentieth century's major conflicts. Nonpolarity need not be equated with chaos.

And so the United States and other leading countries can concentrate on dealing with challenges posed by lesser but still dangerous countries; the threats posed by terrorist groups, drug cartels, and pirates; and the challenges posed by various manifestations of globalization, from pandemic disease to climate change. What is more, it is entirely possible that on occasion the major powers will cooperate in meeting these challenges. China, for example, is something of a limited partner with the United States in reining in some of the worst aspects of North Korean behavior. Both China and Russia work with the United States against terrorism. Also, China and the Soviet Union did not prevent (and on occasion supported) the US and international effort in frustrating and ultimately reversing the 1990 Iraqi invasion and occupation of Kuwait. There was considerable international support for the humanitarian intervention in Libya in 2011. Cooperation in the trade realm is fairly extensive.

None of this could be assumed to occur. There were reasons (often cited by international relations theorists of the realist school) for forecasting as inevitable the end of what was often described as American unipolarity.[2] Great powers, when they act as great powers are wont to do, stimulate competition from others that fear or resent them. This was the history of the seventeenth through twentieth centuries, the era of the modern states system. But while anti-Americanism is identifiable, no great power rival or set of rivals has emerged, or appears likely to emerge over the next decade or two, to challenge the United States.

It is worth focusing on this departure from history. One explanation stems from American strength and the disparity between American power and that of anyone else. The gap in quality and quantity of advanced armaments is so great that it would be unrealistic and self-defeating for China or Russia or any country to take on the United States in the conventional, classic military realm. Nuclear weapons introduce an additional factor that favors caution and restraint; there are few if any differences that warrant all-out war.

To be sure, over the next few decades, China is likely to possess a GDP comparable to and, at one point, greater than that of the United States. But much of that wealth will necessarily be absorbed by providing for China's enormous and, in many cases, still impoverished population, and will not be as available as it otherwise might to fund military development or external undertakings. The same is even more so for India. The EU already possesses a GDP of comparable scale to that of the United States, but the EU does not act in the concerted fashion of a nation-state. Nor is it able or inclined to act in the assertive fashion of historic great powers. Contemporary Japan, for its part, lacks the political culture to play this role. Russia may be more inclined, but its power is limited to nuclear weapons and energy resources. It has little useable military power and is saddled by a declining population and internal challenges to its cohesion. None has the power to overthrow the existing international order.

But the fact that classic great power rivalry has not come to pass, and is unlikely to any time soon, also reflects the truth that the United States has not acted in a way that has stimulated such a response. Yes, doubts about the wisdom and legitimacy of US foreign policy are pervasive, but this tends to lead more to denunciations and head-shaking and to an absence of cooperation than to outright resistance. The world's most powerful countries may not always agree with the United States, but only sometimes do they see America as implacably hostile or as an impediment to their core objectives. In addition, each is to a significant extent preoccupied with its own domestic economic, social, and political challenges. Each has a stake in cooperating to at least some degree on dealing with shared regional and global challenges. What the United States does and seeks to accomplish in the world may not always be welcomed or supported by others, but neither is it normally viewed as a threat to their core or vital national interests. This view reflects a reaction to both what the United States does in the world and how it does it.

And finally, more than ever, the major powers are dependent on the international system for their own economic welfare and political stability and are thus disinclined to attempt to disrupt an order that serves their national purposes. They rely on cross-border flows of goods, services, people, energy, investment, and technology—all of which deeply involves the United States. Interdependence in the modern world is a bulwark (although not a guarantee) against major power competition and conflict. China and the other major and rising powers of the world seek less to overthrow the existing international order than to join it or something resembling it. US relations with the principal new powers of this era (such as Brazil, India, Vietnam, Indonesia, and South Africa) are for the most part good—or at least good enough. They are more interested in integration, even if on somewhat revised terms, than in revolution.

There are also some grounds for optimism at the regional level. Europe, as already discussed, is at peace, its major countries stable and reconciled. Asia has been relatively stable, despite a level of economic dynamism that has historically proved disruptive, some heavy-handed Chinese diplomacy, and the absence of extensive regional arrangements comparable to those that exist in Europe. Latin America is mostly characterized by economic growth, open societies, and peace. Mexico, despite the problems linked to drugs, is thriving economically and democratic politically. Brazil, Colombia, and Chile are impressive by many yardsticks. There are, of course, exceptions, but Cuba, Venezuela, Nicaragua, and a few other countries are just that, exceptions. Africa resists generalization, but a good many countries there are enjoying considerable stability, robust economic growth, and greater political accountability. Again, there are exceptions (including Sudan, Zimbabwe, the Democratic Republic of the Congo, and possibly Nigeria), but the overall pattern is fairly good and certainly better than almost anyone would have predicted a decade ago.

Reason for Worry

We are not about to enter a Kantian period of perpetual peace. Conflicts between various powers cannot be ruled out, either by design (say, over territory, resources, or changes in political status) or by accident. But conflicts on a large scale are unlikely, mostly because of the direct and indirect costs that would accrue to all. Far more likely, however, will be threats to peace and stability caused by the ambitions of select medium-size states, such as North Korea and Iran, that are willing and able to use force to achieve their ambitions, be they regime survival or regional influence or both, and by the consequences of weak states.

North Korea is the most militarized, unfree, and closed-off country on the planet. It also has a handful of nuclear weapons and is developing long-range missiles to carry them. North Korea poses multiple threats to the region and the world in addition to the physical threat it poses to its own citizens, millions of whom have died because of malnutrition. One threat is the direct military threat to South Korea. North Korea could try, as it did in 1950, to unify the peninsula by force, possibly because it feared that the passage of time was working against its interests, given the South's much higher rate of growth. Or the North could once again undertake a small attack (possibly in an effort to shore up the political position of its leadership) that could lead to an exchange that escalated into an all-out conflict. A related scenario could be triggered more by the economic and political collapse of the North than by provocation: Refugees could start to flee in large numbers toward the border with South. The pressure for the United States to intervene militarily under any of these scenarios would be great, given both the stakes and US treaty obligations.

Iran is, in some ways, an even more dangerous and difficult threat to contend with, in part because there is no equivalent of a China prepared to exercise even a modicum of influence over it.[1] Iran is an imperial power on a regional scale. Through the use of proxies, subsidies, ideology, and violence, it has acquired significant influence throughout the greater Middle East—and significant ability to undermine stability and help shape politics in a number of countries, including Iraq, Saudi Arabia, Afghanistan, Bahrain, Syria, and Lebanon.

The most pressing challenge, however, stems from Iran's effort to put into place many of the elements of a nuclear weapons program. It is impossible at this point to know whether Iran's leadership has decided to acquire nuclear weapons or to "park" its program just short of that in the hopes it would then be in a position to derive the lion's share of the benefits of possessing such weapons and avoid most of the risks and costs. Either way, a nuclear or near-nuclear Iran with either an actual or "threshold" nuclear weapons capability would pose a major national security challenge to a range of US interests. It would constitute a threat to Israel and make Iran all the more likely to press to shape the region in its anti-American image. In addition, Iran might be tempted to transfer nuclear weapons or materials to groups such as Hezbollah. And an Iran armed with nuclear weapons, or close to it, might stimulate other countries in the vicinity to follow suit, thereby creating a situation of enormous instability and potential destructiveness.

The United States, together with a handful of other countries, has sought to frustrate Iran's progress both directly (e.g., through clandestine efforts to introduce computer viruses that play havoc with centrifuges) and indirectly (using sanctions that raise the economic costs of proceeding with the program). Against this backdrop, negotiations have started that seek to produce an outcome that is enough for Iran's leaders to accept and not too much for the United States, Israel, and others; it is not at all certain such an outcome can be negotiated.

It is hardly surprising that a great deal of attention is being devoted to the likely direct and indirect consequences of a preventive military strike on Iran's nuclear facilities by the United States, Israel, or both. What is unknown is exactly what such a strike would accomplish in the way of delaying the emergence of an Iranian nuclear weapons program; also unknowable is how Iran would retaliate and with what effect on the stability of neighboring states or on a world economy so dependent on Middle East energy. The danger, of course, is that Iran would retaliate against shipping or other producers, in the process causing an increase in world oil prices that could push much of the world back into recession. Iran would also likely work to rebuild its nuclear program, quite possibly without many of the sanctions or inspections now in place. The regime might also end up stronger as there could well be a "rally around the flag" effect at home; the region, already experiencing considerable turbulence, might become that much more politically unstable.

The alternative would be to live with an Iranian weapon or near-weapon. The United States could make clear to Iran's leaders the enormous price they and their country would pay for the use, a threat to use, or transfer of a nuclear weapon to others. The United States could also extend security guarantees to Iran's neighbors, thereby reducing their incentive to develop or acquire nuclear weapons of their own. Missile defense in the region could be increased. And the United States could increase economic sanctions and try through a variety of mechanisms to foster a change in regime; the same weapons in the hands of more moderate individuals would not constitute the same alarm. One problem is that none of us can be certain that this Iranian regime in possession of nuclear weapons would prove to be rational and responsible; another is that regime change is far easier to hope for than bring about.

Choosing between launching a preventive strike or living with an Iranian nuclear weapons capability would obviously be a fateful choice for any American president and his advisers; that said, they might not have the option to choose were Israel to take matters into its own hands and launch a preventive strike of its own. Israel, given the unique history of the Jewish people and its concentrated population, along with verbal threats to annihilate Israel emanating from Iran's leadership, is highly reluctant to trust its security to deterrence; for understandable reasons, the phrase "mutually assured destruction" does not translate easily into Hebrew. Were Israel to act, the United States would want to do all it could to limit Iran's reaction, making it clear it would pay a far higher price if it acted in a manner that drew the United States into the conflict.

A different set of problems stems from weak states: those unable to meet their responsibilities to fellow states and to their own citizens and that as a result pose a threat to both.

One way of demonstrating weakness is through an inability to assert sovereign control over national territory. Where states cannot do this, terrorists, drug cartels, pirates, and other criminal enterprises can thrive. This is different than a government's choosing to associate itself with such enterprises, something that makes it and its country an outlaw state. Afghanistan before and at the time of 9/11 was an outlaw state in that the Taliban leadership of the day elected to provide al-Qaeda with sanctuary and other support. This is different from Afghanistan today, which is more of a weak state, one that simply lacks the means to make sure its territory is not used by terrorists. This is a distinction with a difference, although state failure to meet its obligations can provide a justification for intervention in one form or another, even if the failure stems from a lack of capacity rather than policy.

As for how weak states can also pose threats to others, take Pakistan. It is possible to debate whether Pakistan is best understood as an outlaw state or a weak one; in reality, it is both. Its association with terrorism reflects both weakness and choice. Pakistan's government lacks the capacity to deny terrorists any use of its territory, but it is also true that elements of Pakistan's security establishment either support what select terrorists are doing or look the other way. What makes this all the more disconcerting is that Pakistan possesses a sizable and growing arsenal of nuclear weapons, now estimated to number more than one hundred. As a result, it constitutes one of the greatest threats to stability and safety in the world. US policy should continue to adjust accordingly; all assistance should be made strictly conditional on Pakistani behavior, and where necessary (as was the case in the raid that killed Osama bin Laden) the United States should act independently, even at the risk of introducing further strain into an increasingly strained relationship.

Weak states can also cause damage in other realms. Indonesia and Brazil are not always in a position to prevent the deforestation of significant areas of their respective countries, thereby exacerbating climate change. Indonesia and other states cannot police rural areas adequately to maintain health standards, the result being the emergence of exotic and dangerous forms of influenza in farm animals that are carried through them to the human population. Today's global world is unlike the advertised Las Vegas: What happens anywhere does not stay there. It is only a matter of time (and often not a lot of it) before the consequences of weakness in the most remote areas become global.

The best option for the United States is prevention, to either keep a weak state from getting weaker or to shore up a state that is already weak. This involves providing economic aid to deal with pressing humanitarian needs and to promote sustainable development through extending support to governments willing to adopt the political, economic, and social policies known to attract investment and generate economic growth. It may also require training, advising, and arming national or local police forces to deal with internal challenges to stability and the country's army or coast guard to deal with external threats. The United States may need to carry out certain security-related functions itself, especially if the threats are developed. If this all sounds like nation-building lite, absent the large military footprint, it is because it is. But it is just this modesty of effort on the part of the United States that makes such undertakings affordable and in line with expected benefits.

The Middle East Morass

US interests in the Middle East are greater than American influence there. That, in a nutshell, is the current predicament of the United States. What adds to it is the region's continuing turmoil. The Middle East is akin to a geological region beset by multiple fault lines, defined by frequent wars, seemingly insoluble conflicts, the potential spread of nuclear materials, terrorism, weak regional institutions, and limited political legitimacy and hence stability within many of its countries.

Politically speaking, the Middle East is the least successful region of the world. It is a patchwork quilt of top-heavy monarchies, authoritarian regimes trying to hang on, sectarian strife, unresolved conflicts between and among states, regional rivalries, and nationalities that cross and contest boundaries.

The old order in the Middle East, one largely built on authoritarian regimes often willing to work with the United States on behalf of one or more regional interests, is either gone or shaken. Change is taking place rapidly. The emerging Middle East is a region of governments of uncertain orientation and limited capacities. There are few boundaries between the religious and the political; to the contrary, dominant political parties and movements are to one degree or another promoting an Islamic agenda.

What can and should the United States do? Washington needs to be mindful that the alternatives to a flawed authoritarian regime can be worse. Democracy is no panacea, and democracies in the Middle East are certain to be anything but mature democracies for decades to come, if ever. Immature democracies with at most limited checks on consolidated power and weak traditions of compromise have a history of treating both their own people and their neighbors badly.[1] As a rule, it is preferable to promote evolutionary political change over the revolutionary; where this is impossible, the US approach to new regimes that emerge should be highly conditional. Assistance and support for international loans should be linked in part to how governments act at home and abroad; diplomatic presence should depend upon governments meeting their obligation to provide security. Where governments are unwilling or unable to fulfill their international obligations (e.g., against terrorists), the United States should work with them to develop such capacities but also reserve the right to act independently if need be. Highly conditional, at times transactional relationships will fast become the norm throughout the region for the United States.

What makes all this so relevant and disconcerting is that the region's turmoil has the potential to affect not just the peoples and countries of the Middle East but, owing to globalization, the entire world. One critical interest is energy—the region possesses more than half the world's known oil and produces more than a third of global output. Although US imports and consumption of Middle East oil are relatively modest—the United States gets only 20 percent of its oil imports and 10 percent of the oil it consumes from the region—Middle East production is central to the global oil market and global economy on which the United States depends. In addition, the region produces and is home to many of the world's most dangerous terrorists. Nuclear proliferation and the threat posed by Iran's ambitions are other vital concerns, as is Israel's security.

For decades, much of the world's interest in the region centered on the conflict between Israel and its neighbors. It was widely believed that progress in this context was central to the region's future. It was a belief that was exaggerated. Anger and frustration over the absence of a Palestinian state did not trigger the upheavals in the Arab world. Nor was it central to 9/11, Saddam Hussein's invasion of Kuwait, or the increase in Sunni-Shia and Arab-Iranian tensions. Don't get me wrong: There is a strong case to be made for the creation of a capable, responsible Palestinian state, in part because it would bolster Israel's ability to remain secure, prosperous, democratic, and Jewish, and also because it would bolster America's standing in the region and much of the world. But achieving peace will not be easy no matter what the American diplomatic effort; what is more, resolving the Palestinian issue and bringing about peace with Israel would not resolve the region's many ills even if peace were somehow to come about.

In fact, what modest progress that has been realized over the past four decades through the Middle East peace process is not assured to survive the still-to-be-determined political futures of Egypt and Syria. Also unpredictable is the future orientation and leadership of traditional monarchies, including Jordan, one of the two Arab countries to have entered into a formal peace agreement with Israel. The same holds for the political balance between more moderate, secular Palestinians who dominate the West Bank and the more radical Hamas, which controls Gaza, and the political landscape inside Israel.

It is much too soon to conclude that recent political developments in the region will change much or possibly any of this favorably; indeed, the era of peacemaking between leaders is over. Peace must henceforth be supported by the masses and by elected politicians loyal to parties and populations heavily influenced by religion. This may make any peace accord sturdier once it is in place—but it will also make it much more difficult to arrive at peace in the first instance. But peace (and certainly a lasting peace) is not something that can be imposed. For peace to have a chance, national leaders must be able and willing to take political risks and compromise, traits not in abundance in this region or likely to be any time soon.

The Consequences of History's Return

Many of the predictions that greeted the end of the Cold War proved to be both overly optimistic and short-lived. But to say that history has returned is not to argue that history as we knew it has returned. Some important things are different: the unprecedented distribution of power in the world; the reality of globalization, along with a large gap between the forces it has unleashed and the arrangements meant to manage them; a significant and growing degree of interdependence; and the widespread availability of modern information and communications technology.

Great power competition and conflict will not be the primary source of turmoil in the next few decades. This is not to say there won't be flare-ups or even that armed conflict is inconceivable. But for now, this is a world mostly ready to live with American primacy. None of the major powers has as yet the capacity or inclination to challenge America's lead. The major powers also benefit from external order and the economic interactions it allows, something that tends to introduce a degree of caution into their foreign policies. Instead, the principal challenges to world order come from the gap between globalization's challenges and the arrangements meant to deal with them, a dynamic Asia whose economic success is threatened by growing nationalism, a turbulent and violent Middle East, select medium-size powers that reject the status quo, and weak states that are unable or unwilling to meet their basic obligations to their own citizens and their neighbors.

We are also entering a period in which the nature of global alignments will be much more volatile and fluid than they were, say, during the Cold War. The alliance systems that provided the foundation for much of what went on—NATO and the Warsaw Pact—were built around predictable threats, likely scenarios, and specific obligations. But precisely these characteristics are in short supply in a world of shifting threats, differing perceptions, and societies with widely divergent readiness to maintain and use military force. Unpredictability will make alliances far more difficult to depend on; much more likely is episodic cooperation among select allies. For better and for worse, relationships are about to become much more à la carte than anything blanket.

This is not all bad; fewer countries will prove to be reflexive or sworn adversaries. What President Obama said in response to a question in September 2012 about Egypt's new government—"I don't think that we would consider them an ally, but we don't consider them an enemy"—could just as easily be said about a good many other countries.[1] There is a potential for cooperation on a limited, selective basis. Countries will be partners on some issues, opponents on some, and bystanders on still others. We are already seeing cooperation (albeit limited) between the United States and both China and Russia, when it comes to the Iranian and North Korean nuclear programs.

Adversaries may be able to cooperate on other global issues, ranging from counterterrorism and trade to climate change and disease; for example, even the United States and Iran cooperated for a time in Afghanistan and the United States and Cuba have worked together on combatting illegal drugs. But we should not kid ourselves: Such cooperation with adversaries will be the exception. All things being equal, greater unpredictability in the world will make designing and conducting foreign policy more difficult.

Lord Palmerston's dictum—Nations have no permanent friends nor permanent enemies, only permanent interests—is likely to find a new lease on life two centuries after it was first pronounced. The challenge for diplomacy will be to enlist cooperation that is both broad and deep—and to insulate relationships so that inevitable disagreements and disappointments do not spill over and make cooperation impossible when it should not be. The twenty-first century promises to be a demanding environment in which to make policy. Indeed, the premium on a smart and nimble foreign policy has arguably never been greater.

Part II

Restoration Abroad

The message of this book is that the United States, while in a unique position to do some valuable things in the world, cannot do everything. It certainly cannot continue doing the same things in the same way either at home or abroad. What is needed is nothing less than a new approach to both domestic and foreign policy; changing just one would be desirable but insufficient. The stakes could hardly be greater: the nature of the twenty-first century and the prosperity and security of the United States. What is more, the two are intimately intertwined: Americans will not enjoy the standard of living or quality of life they aspire to at home amid chaos abroad—and the United States will not be in a position to limit chaos abroad unless it rebuilds the foundations of its strength at home.

The world is likely to provide an opportunity to do just this. As the first half of this book made clear, there is no existing threat on the order of a Nazi Germany or a Soviet Union; in other words, a country or group of countries with the capacity and ideology to confront the United States. Nor is there likely

81

to be one for some time. Whatever challenges and threats exist (and they surely do exist) tend to be either structural—a lack of machinery and cooperation to meet the problems intrinsic to globalization—or, in one way or another, limited in their impact, including North Korea, Iran, and any number of weak states, such as Pakistan. Nothing rises to the level of existential, although terrorism involving nuclear material and weapons has the potential to come uncomfortably close to that threshold. The odds are good that the challenges (or their consequences) can be managed or contained even if the basic problem cannot be resolved or eliminated.

This is not an invitation for the United States to do nothing in or about the world, but it is an opportunity that allows this country to be more selective in what it does (and how it does it) overseas and to focus more attention and resources on what it is doing at home. The objective must be to take advantage of the opportunity—think of it as a strategic respite—to restore the foundations of American power, including the economy, schools, infrastructure, and so on. The goal is to increase the number of Americans who can hold their own in an increasingly competitive global marketplace, shore up the economic and physical resilience of the country, and ensure that sufficient resources are available so that the United States can do what it wants and needs to do both at home and abroad.

What should define and guide American foreign policy in such a setting? It is not a new question; to the contrary, it has been with us for a generation, ever since the end of the Cold War and the demise of containment, the doctrine that made the case for pushing back against the spread of Soviet power and influence. Containment could not survive its own success—in the end, the United States and its allies not only resisted Soviet expansion but helped bring about the unraveling of both the Soviet empire and the Soviet Union itself—but as a foreign policy doctrine it is, at best, of marginal relevance to the post–Cold War world. Absent the emergence of an overarching threat, what is needed is a doctrine that helps determine what it is the United States favors, as much as what it opposes.[1]

Multilateralism—collective, coordinated action by states and sometimes others—is sometimes put forward as a doctrine, but in reality is more a means for implementing whatever foreign policy is ultimately embraced. Doctrines are about objectives, the purposes of policy. Multilateralism is not an end in itself, so much as a means. It is about execution, no more and no less.

This does not make multilateralism unimportant. It is anything but, if only because implementation accounts for a lot in life. At a minimum, multilateralism offers up a mechanism for burden-sharing, a way by which the United States can distribute among others the costs of a particular course of action. Second, multilateralism is often an essential element of a policy, in that global problems tend to require broad-based responses. Even a few outliers can undermine a sanction designed to thwart nuclear proliferation or an international agreement meant to promote trade, slow climate change, or stem the spread of disease. Third, multilateralism can increase the willingness of other governments and peoples to accept a policy; it can add to the legitimacy of what is being done. The United States does not need the world's permission to act, but it does often need the world's support to succeed.

In principle, one could live with having no foreign policy doctrine, either because it is too hard to come up with one that fits the realities of the world or because a doctrine may be viewed as more of a luxury than a necessity. It is also fair to say that no framework can be expected to provide guidance to every foreign policy choice; even containment was unable to do this.

Nevertheless, a foreign policy doctrine serves useful purposes. It can provide overall policy direction and help establish priorities. Doctrine can help shape, size, and steer the allocation of resources. And a doctrine can send useful signals to allies and adversaries, and to the public and Congress. For the pressed policymaker, the intellectual framework provided by a doctrine is far preferable to improvisation.

Doctrines and Democracy

The promotion of democracy is a perennial choice of many across the political spectrum when it comes to selecting a foreign policy compass. For a century, Democratic and Republican administrations alike have, to varying degrees, embraced the spread of democracy as a foreign policy objective. It is consistent with American values and a necessary precondition of the democratic peace, the idea that mature democracies treat not only their own citizens better but their neighbors as well. Democracies also tend to be more resilient than alternatives; they may suffer from all sorts of uncertainties, but are much less prone to revolutionary changes than are more brittle authoritarian or totalitarian systems.[1]

Democracy promotion is something different and more fundamental than the promotion of human rights, which for decades during the Cold War was a staple of American foreign policy, in particular during the administrations of Jimmy Carter and Ronald Reagan. The spread of democracy was central to the foreign policy of George W. Bush, both rhetorically—his second inaugural stated that "America's vital interests and our deepest beliefs are now one"—and actually: The Iraq war was launched in part to create a democratic Iraq, something that was predicted to be a model the rest of the region would be unable to resist. Democracy promotion also occupies a conspicuous if inconsistent space in the foreign policy of Barack Obama, as evidenced most in his approach to the Middle East.

There are, however, several problems with a foreign policy that places a priority on spreading democracy. One is the reality that it can be difficult; there is no cookbook with recipes to use. As we are seeing in the Middle East, it is one thing to oust authoritarian regimes, something very different and more difficult to replace them with something demonstrably and enduringly better. Such phrases as "democratic revolution" and "Arab Spring" and "getting on the right side of history" are widely employed, but what is unfolding is anything but certain to lead to genuine democracies or peace or even political outcomes better than what existed. Iraq and Afghanistan are both cautionary tales here as well. It is not just that the costs of occupation and nation-building are too great to be a template for what the United States might do elsewhere, it is also that even with a decade of American occupation and nation-building, not all that much in the way of democratic institutions (not to mention viable societies) exists in these countries. There is also the real-world complication of the need to work with nondemocracies to achieve other pressing foreign policy goals. Active promotion of democracy can get in the way of cooperation on other matters, ranging from counterterrorism and conflict resolution to thwarting proliferation and financing deficits. Relations with Russia and China are obviously examples of just this.

It has become commonplace in recent years to suggest that the United States erred in the Middle East by not doing more to promote democratic reform. Most famous was the criticism made in Cairo in 2005 by Secretary of State Condoleezza Rice:

"For sixty years, the United States pursued stability at the expense of democracy in the Middle East—and we achieved neither."[2] But this criticism needs to be tempered. First, the United States enjoyed (and in certain cases continues to enjoy) decades of cooperation with nondemocratic governments in the Middle East. There are good results to show for these relationships, including meaningful progress toward peace between Israel and several of its neighbors, regular access to plentiful amounts of oil and gas, and concerted efforts against acts of cross-border aggression and terrorism. Sure, it would have been preferable to have had all that and democratic reform, too, but it simply wasn't in the cards. It is more than a little difficult to persuade governments to cooperate on issues that matter to you at the same time you are perceived as working to undermine them. Indeed, when it comes to the Middle East, promoting democratic reform qualifies as *an* interest of the United States, but hardly the only one. The United States also wants to frustrate the proliferation of weapons of mass destruction, ensure Israeli security, promote progress toward peace between Israel and its neighbors, create an environment in which fewer young men and women become terrorists and that those who do cannot operate freely, and assure ample oil and gas production and the ability to export it.

Experience also demonstrates that it is easier to press for democracy than bring it about. I know firsthand from my time in the White House and State Department that numerous American officials (myself included) tried it with Egypt. We made some progress on the economic side, (e.g., in persuading the government to open up the country to foreign investment) but little on the political, as Hosni Mubarak resisted what he saw as well-intentioned but naive calls for change. Reform can rarely be forced or imposed on an unwilling friend; indeed, it is often more difficult to pressure friends and allies than adversaries. (One exception to this rule may have been Iran under Mohammad Reza Shah Pahlavi, where the United States had the leverage to press for political and economic reforms and held off until it was too late. But such situations, where the friend needs the United States incomparably more than Washington needs them, tend to be rare.) Sanctions or threatening to distance ourselves from Mubarak's Egypt by cutting off military and economic aid was not a real option, due to the US stake in Egyptian-Israeli peace, shared opposition to the threats posed by Saddam Hussein's Iraq and revolutionary Iran, and counterterrorism cooperation. Distancing ourselves from the anything but democratic or tolerant Saudi Arabia was and is not viable, due to world dependence on Saudi oil production and exports or, in the past, the priority given to cooperation against the Soviet Union in Afghanistan.

This is not an argument for going to the other extreme and remaining silent on matters of political reform. But US officials, before pushing for improved respect for human rights or more fundamental political change, need to assess the potential for such change given local realities, the policy instruments available, and the indirect and direct costs that would accrue to the United States for trying, including this country's reputation for reliability and loyalty to its friends. It makes little sense to make a big push for reform if the prospects are poor and the United States would pay an enormous price in the process; in other circumstances, however, there may be opportunity to effect desirable change at little expense. A common, consistent policy is not in the cards.

More specifically, US officials should normally speak truth to power in private, making the case for the sort of responsible reform that history has proven enhances political stability and promotes economic growth. There may be occasion for reiterating criticism in public, but this should be done only if it is likely to make the situation better rather than simply make officials feel better. The United States should provide financial and other support to civil society groups, offer political support to courageous individuals who stand up to a regime's worst elements, and monitor elections. If relevant, economic assistance should be offered to the government in question as an incentive and revoked (or threatened to be revoked) if there is reason to believe that doing so would have the desired effect. It is obviously the sovereign right of other governments and countries to design and carry out their own political and economic arrangements. But it is no less the sovereign right of the United States to offer or withhold economic aid, to support or oppose the extension of financial assistance from international institutions, or to put forward or withhold incentives and guarantees for investment. Conditionalism, rather than blank checks, ought to guide what the US government is prepared to do.

It needs to be emphasized, too, that democracy is about more than elections and that elections are about more than what happens on election day. The run-up to elections—the willingness to allow the political opposition equal access to influential media and to organize—can be more important. Indeed, what matters most in a democracy is a willingness to lose elections, not have them. Democracy also needs to be about much more than majority rule; it needs to be equally protective of minority rights. Constitutionalism, along with real checks and balances, be it among the branches of government or between government and society, is vital, as is the development of a truly independent civil society. The United States did itself no favor by pressing as hard and as early as it did for elections in Gaza; premature elections, in this instance bringing to power an armed, intolerant, and illiberal force such as Hamas, can work against the cause of both democracy and peace.

Some final points. No single path or pace or sequence (including the relationship between political and economic reform) defines what makes for a true democracy or an acceptable political outcome. As is the case with driving, speed can be dangerous. More generally, the ideal can all too easily become the enemy of the possible and the good. Second, the United States may want to accept a political role for military leaders during times of political transition. The army is often the most professional and respected institution in developing countries, one with a good deal of public support. Third, Americans need to be hard-headed and keep in mind the Hippocratic oath of doing no harm. The alternative to a less than democratic but friendly government can be a less than democratic but hostile government. Iran under the shah versus Iran under the ayatollahs comes to mind here. Hopefully, Egypt will not come to be an additional example. The United States may soon have to decide how to react to internal challenges to such long-term friends as the leaders of Jordan, Bahrain, Morocco, and, eventually, Saudi Arabia. One can only hope that abstractions and optimism do not overwhelm assessments of national interests and realities and that policymakers hold opposition leaders and movements to the same standards used for governments. Last, US officials need to keep in mind that Western-style democracy, with its separation of powers and checks and balances, divide between church and state, and protection of individual liberties and minority rights, may not be universal in its appeal or reach. This is not to demonstrate "the soft bigotry of low expectations" so much as to acknowledge the power of local culture, tradition, and history.

Saving Lives

Humanitarianism is another contender for what should most guide US efforts around the world, one that dominated much of the efforts of the Clinton administration (in Somalia, Haiti, Bosnia, Kosovo) and more recently led to American support for and participation in the intervention in Libya. The same issue was at the core of the subsequent debate about Syria.

The appeal of humanitarianism is obvious: to save innocent life. Alas, there is no shortage of situations calling out for such intervention. But therein also lies part of the problem with humanitarianism: its almost unlimited call on American resources at a time when US economic and military resources are strained. Moreover, addressing the root causes of humanitarian crises can require long-term capacity or nation-building, an even more demanding and expensive proposition. In many instances, vital US interests are nowhere to be found. Also, humanitarianism provides no guidance to what the United States should be prepared to do in a host of other situations in which US interests may be vital or where a problem or crisis may be political, economic, or strategic rather than humanitarian in nature. In the end, it is too narrow and too divorced from strategic interests to serve as a foreign policy doctrine.

Still, what to do when humanitarian crises emerge is an unavoidable issue. It helps to have a template, a set of questions, which would inform any decision as to whether, as well as how, to get involved in an actual or potential humanitarian crisis. The United States should be wary of armed humanitarian interventions except in those circumstances where the threat is both large and not in doubt, the potential victims have requested help, the opposition (and alternative) to the government is judged to be both viable and committed to objectives deemed acceptable to this country, there is substantial international support and participation in the mission, there is a high likelihood of success at a limited cost, and other policies are judged to be inadequate. There also needs to be an assessment of competing claims on US resources and the greater context; that is, whether it is necessary to keep one's powder dry for other pressing contingencies. With these stringent criteria, the scales will more often than not tilt against direct military intervention.

Libya met some but not all of these tests. There were indigenous requests for help, and regional and international support for doing something. Libya looked to be a decent bet: It was a country of low population density and with relatively weak pro-government forces. But it was not clear that Mu'ammar Gadhafi was going to make good on his verbal threats against those who had taken up arms against him. The United States had at most a limited stake in the country's future. Also uncertain was the orientation of the opposition. And there may have been the unexpected cost of reinforcing the perceived value of nuclear weapons, as other rulers might well conclude that the Libyan regime (like Saddam's before it) made itself vulnerable to Western military intervention when it abandoned its nuclear

program. Although the limited intervention by several European countries and the United States succeeded in ousting a
repressive and at times violent regime, the killing of the American ambassador in Benghazi in September 2012 suggests it is
premature to have confidence in Libya's future or to assess the
full consequences of the intervention, including the spreading
of arms from Libya to other African countries.[1]

The Syrian case is even more complex. The human tragedy
is great; many tens of thousands of men, women, and children
have lost their lives. Additionally, a strategic case can be made
for ousting a government so close to Iran. But the Syrian opposition is divided and to an unknown extent embraces an agenda
the United States cannot support. Regional and international
opposition to intervening on behalf of antigovernment forces
is considerable. This reality, along with the strength of government forces and the sectarian nature of Syrian society, guarantees that any intervention would have to be large scale and
prolonged to have any prospect of succeeding. It would be hard
to justify undertaking so potentially costly an intervention at a
time when the United States needs to be ready for a possible
conflict with Iran, maintain greater presence in the Asia-Pacific,
and reduce the deficit.

To raise such questions is not to argue for turning one's back
on human suffering, be it from natural causes or man-made.
This country should not, for reasons of principle and calculation alike. The American reputation for morality and leadership alike suffers when the US government chooses to stand by
rather than act amid images of atrocities. But humanitarian intervention should not be equated with or limited to direct military intervention; in particular, intervention with ground forces.
A host of potential responses may prove a viable alternative,
including economic and political sanctions against offending

governments, provision of nonlethal and lethal aid to oppositionists, covert action, and diplomatic initiatives. In the direct military realm, there is a full menu ranging from providing advisers and trainers or establishing and enforcing no-fly and no-drive zones to providing air support of select local forces or introducing "boots on the ground." There are also more narrow humanitarian options, such as establishing and protecting safe-havens for refugees or internally displaced persons, when the aim is simply to keep people alive rather than alter the political or military context. Any number of these could have had a positive effect in both Libya and Syria.

Efforts to come up with a consistent policy for humanitarian crises are doomed to fail and misguided, because of the multiple criteria that need to guide the reaction to a given situation. The international community has enshrined the "Responsibility to Protect" (R2P) as an obligation of all states to fulfill on behalf of threatened peoples everywhere. But a one-size-fits-all-situations standard is impractical and ill-advised. This reality argues for revisiting the entire concept, as protection may be too high a bar in particular circumstances. The United States would be better served by adopting a "Responsibility to Respond"—R2R, if you will—but this would be something fundamentally different in concept and application alike. Reaction could take the form of actions against the government or on behalf of those being threatened or killed, but depending on circumstances, the response could and sometimes would amount to less than full protection. Here and elsewhere in foreign policy, inconsistency can be a virtue.

Taking on Terrorists

Counterterrorism, a third possible foreign policy doctrine, understandably gained currency in the aftermath of 9/11. Why it is an element of US national security policy is self-evident. Terrorists constitute a threat to American interests worldwide as well as to the homeland; this country's servicemen, diplomats, businessmen, and tourists are all vulnerable. So, too, are governments that work with the United States and societies that share many of its values. Terrorism can be an effective tool of the weak; as we saw on 9/11, a relatively small investment can have an enormous payoff in what it can destroy. Open societies such as the United States are especially vulnerable.

Like humanitarianism, counterterrorism is more defined by what it is against than by what it favors. Also like humanitarianism, it can be carried out on a tactical level, to deal with a particular manifestation of the problem, or strategically, to deal with the root causes.

Dealing with root causes can involve a number of approaches in this realm. All are ambitious. One would require remaking other countries, often beginning with a change of regime, so that the government comes to treat terrorists as an adversary.

This is what has been attempted by the United States in Afghanistan. It required combined intelligence and military options to oust the regime, followed by more than a decade of nation-building. The problem with this approach is its high cost and low likelihood of success.

A variant of this approach has been tried with Iran. Sanctions have been put in place to make the regime pay a price for its support of terrorism, with the hope that the regime will come to judge the price as too high and therefore pull back from supporting terror. Unfortunately, the regime has determined that the benefits of employing terrorism as an instrument of domestic and foreign policy outweigh the costs. Energy exports give the regime a good deal of latitude to resist external pressures. What is more, the United States does not have the luxury of conducting a foreign policy toward Iran solely on the basis of terrorism; that policy must also balance carrots and sticks to influence Iranian policy vis-à-vis its nuclear program, Iraq, Afghanistan, and much else.

A different approach to opposing terrorism is to try to nip it in the bud, by discouraging young men and women from becoming terrorists in the first place, or to reinvent themselves and become a former terrorist if they joined up at one point in their lives. This is a worthy aim, one that should be pursued, not so much as an alternative to other policies than as a complement. It means changing what is preached in the mosque, taught in the school, read on the Internet, and discussed in the home. It requires influential people in the society and communities in question to speak out and work in every way possible to discourage and, more important, delegitimize terrorism as an acceptable way of pursuing a political agenda. All of this will take decades, at best. What is more, by definition such things cannot be mandated or controlled; the prospects for this approach are modest by its being both indirect and retail.[1]

Terrorism can also be fought at the tactical level. This involves targeting known terrorists with drones or with special forces, much along the lines of what was carried out in Pakistan against Osama bin Laden. This is all warranted, but it is no panacea. Drones cannot always reach their targets, and even when they do, can kill innocents and in the process anger large segments of societies and their governments. There is international legal backing for attacking terrorists on foreign soil (on the grounds that governments unable or unwilling to fulfill their sovereign obligations forfeit some of their sovereign protections), but that does not assuage those who see the strikes as an insulting infringement of sovereignty or as a threat in and of themselves. The danger is that the United States risks alienating the very governments and societies it is seeking to win over. Secretary of Defense Donald Rumsfeld's question—"Are we capturing, killing or deterring and dissuading more terrorists every day than the madrassas and the radical clerics are recruiting, training and deploying against us?"—remains valid.[2] Attacks by Special Forces run similar risks in addition to those they pose to individuals carrying out the mission. Nevertheless, the United States should be prepared to use drones or Special Forces when dangerous, high-value targets are identified, there is a good chance of killing or capturing them, and the host government lacks either the capacity or will to act on its own.

We also need to understand and accept that no amount of counterterrorism can be 100 percent effective. There will always be individuals ready to use violence to promote their political goals. And there will always be governments unable or unwilling to make sure they cannot act. As is the case with fighting disease, no solution is at hand. But a comprehensive approach promises to reduce the scale of the terrorist threat and the costs it inflicts on the American economy and society. All this is one reason why the phrase "war on terrorism" is unhelpful. There is a need to use many tools and not just the military, as well as the reality that one must act everywhere—not just on battlefields and not just against committed identifiable combatants. Terrorism must be counteracted where it exists. The United States, along with like-minded governments, must also try to reduce the pool of recruits, build the capacity of friendly countries, strengthen existing international counterterror machinery, and make it more difficult through active and passive (protective) measures for terrorists to succeed at the tactical level. Yet we also need to accept the reality that on occasion terrorists will succeed despite all that is put in place to thwart them. This underscores the need to make the American society and economy more resilient through such measures as civil defense, first responder training, and redundancy of critical components. The goal is to enhance the capacity of the United States to manage crises in a way that minimizes loss of life and economic disruption and reduces the time it takes to bounce back.

Negotiation might have a limited role in particular circumstances that require persuading "traditional" terrorists to foreswear violence, but that is because their aims are narrow and specific, such as to bring about greater autonomy or a separate country for a people; in such cases, compromise may be possible. But negotiation has no role when the objectives of terrorists are essentially existential, when nothing will do for them short of eliminating what they view as the enemy and returning society to a pure, seventh-century state.

It is just as important not to lose perspective. Terrorists have little global appeal. They can destroy but not create. It is telling that the people who went into the streets of Cairo and other cities of the Middle East in 2011 and 2012 did not do so in the name of al-Qaeda or on behalf of its agenda. The events of 9/11 did not usher in an era dominated by terrorism; to the contrary, the last decade was dominated much more by the wars in Iraq and Afghanistan, the lingering effects of the economic crisis, and by the spread of new mobile technologies. Looking ahead, the ability of Americans to put their house in order, China's trajectory, and the world's ability to contend with globalization—all are more likely to define the future than will terrorism. The United States should take care not to turn its society upside down in the process of making it less vulnerable and more resilient. It needs to stay open for business and true to its values and principles.

At the same time, the country must be serious about just how dangerous is the threat, especially should terrorists gain access to nuclear materials or biological agents. As is often the case, a balance needs be struck. Effective counterterrorism requires that the federal government and law enforcement agencies be given enhanced capacity to monitor plans and activities of citizens and noncitizens alike. Americans need to recognize that the lines between what is domestic and what is foreign may have long traditions and legal standing but that they count for little in a global world in which borders of every sort are crossed with unimaginable frequency. Accepting some limits on what is seen as the right of privacy may be a price well worth paying in return for much-enhanced safety.

It is important to keep perspective in another sense as well. Counterterrorism is too narrow and limited in scope to provide guidance for dealing with many of the challenges and opportunities posed by globalization and this era of international relations. At the end of the day, terrorism is but one challenge on America's plate. Dealing with it is a necessary component of US foreign policy, but cannot be the whole of it or provide a framework.

Integration

Integration is the fourth and final contender for a foreign policy doctrine. Unlike containment, which was about limiting the reach of selected countries, integration is about bringing them in, to make them a part of regional and global arrangements. Integration aims to develop rules and institutions to govern international relations and persuade as many governments as possible to see that these rules are followed and shared objectives are realized. As is the case with democracy promotion, integration represents a "positive" approach to foreign policy, in that it emphasizes a set of objectives to be created rather than frustrated.[1]

But at its core, integration is fundamentally different from democracy promotion. Democracy promotion seeks to change the internal nature of other countries, out of both principle and the belief that democracies will behave better beyond their borders. Integration, by contrast, focuses mostly on what states do beyond their borders. It is a foreign policy that seeks to influence the foreign policies of other countries. Indeed, integration is premised on the idea that international cooperation is possible between democracies and governments that sit on top of relatively closed political and economic systems. The US ability to regulate competition and avoid conflict with the Soviet Union during the Cold War was one example, as is today's US-China relationship. So, too, were Israel's peace with authoritarian Egypt and its peace with the Kingdom of Jordan.

Integration was the implicit underpinning of George H. W. Bush's call for the creation of a "New World Order," an objective for a more cooperative era of relations articulated in the wake of both the Cold War and the successful international collaboration that ousted Saddam Hussein and his army from Kuwait. Elements of integration could be observed in both the Clinton era (such as NAFTA, the US-Canada-Mexico trade deal) and to a lesser extent George W. Bush (global counterterrorism arrangements). Integration enjoyed something of a renaissance in the initial years of the Obama administration; it can be found in the effort to engage broadly with China, "reset" relations with Russia, create a global mechanism to slow climate change, establish a framework for expanded ties with Brazil, and advocate for India gaining a permanent seat in the UN Security Council. Integration is both the argument for and the reflection of both China and Russia's being members of the World Trade Organization.

Integration is highly relevant to the US relationship with China, arguably the most important bilateral relationship now and for the foreseeable future. It remains very much in the interest of the United States and the world that China be integrated into regional and global arrangements to manage the economy, limit climate change, and combat the proliferation of weapons of mass destruction and the means to deliver them long distances. China's help is needed if Korea is ever to be unified peacefully, Iran is to be prevented from gaining nuclear weapons, and Pakistan is to change its ways and not fail. Integration also provides a rationale for the US relationship with China now that its original raison d'être (shared opposition to the spread of Soviet influence) is no longer relevant and its subsequent basis (mutual economic benefit) is too narrow.

Nevertheless, it is just as clear that integration alone cannot inform the entire US approach to China. Talk of a US-Chinese "G-2" or "condominium" is unrealistic. China is not yet ready to become a partner in building and operating regional and global institutions, in part because its leaders remain focused on their perceived internal needs, and in part because this rising power is busy asserting itself throughout the region. The smart policy for the United States and others (as is often the case amid uncertainty) is to hedge: to maintain a strong diplomatic, economic, and military presence in the region and a deep set of ties to local states. Such a stance discourages China from acting aggressively, gives local states confidence to stand up to a much bigger and stronger China, and provides the foundations of a robust response should China all the same embark on a nationalistic, intimidating course. Adopting a policy of containment at this juncture would be premature, however, and could actually help bring about an adversarial relationship that would serve the interests of no one. It is not in the world's interest to isolate China or increase any sense of resentment the Chinese hold. To the contrary, the last thing the world should want to see is a China that seeks to assuage domestic frustration through foreign adventurism.

China's limited embrace of integration is hardly unique. Many other governments are not prepared to sign up to it when it comes to actual policy or, even if they are as a matter of principle, lack the resources to do much for integration in practice. Not surprisingly, world trade talks are stalled; global climate change talks are in even worse shape. Agreement on what to do to denuclearize North Korea, prevent Iran's nuclearization, stop the repression and civil war in Syria, or deal with global economic challenges (despite the G-20) is sharply limited. Why is integration not gaining more traction? The simple answer is that most governments (including the US) are more sensitive to immediate domestic political and economic pressures and interests than they are to medium- and long-term considerations. There are, as well, flat-out disagreements (e.g., no consensus on the extent of or limits to sovereignty, when it is legitimate to use military force, what steps should be taken now to slow climate change), differing priorities, and resource constraints. As was discussed in the previous section, international community is more a goal than a reality. It doesn't mean the United States should give up on it, or fail to advance it when and where possible; incremental gains should be sought and nailed down whenever the opportunities present themselves. But integration alone cannot frame the US relationship with the world. Although the most appealing foreign policy compass for the long term, it is only a partial guide for the here and now.

Restoration

A doctrine exists that fits the circumstances of the United States at this moment in history. It is "Restoration." This new doctrine (which, just to be clear, has nothing to do with Charles II or the English monarchy) rests on several pillars. First, it judges the world to be relatively unthreatening (again, compared to what was experienced in much of the previous century) and makes the most of this situation. Under Restoration, the United States would increase the resources devoted to internal as opposed to international challenges, so as to address critical domestic needs. The aim is to rebuild the foundation of this country's strength to be in a better position to stave off potential strategic rivals or be better prepared for them should they emerge all the same. Second, a foreign policy informed by Restoration would eschew a foreign policy focus on the greater Middle East and any more large-scale land wars for the purpose of remaking other societies. Instead, the priority of US foreign policy would be to shape the behavior of the other principal powers. In addition, US attention and effort would be more broadly distributed—in particular, to the Asia-Pacific region, the part of the world most likely to influence the course of this century. US attention would also be directed more to the Western Hemisphere. This is consistent with both the region's centrality to America's economic and energy future and the reality that stability in Mexico and in the Western Hemisphere more broadly is of vital importance to America's own security. Third, Restoration would rebalance the implementation of foreign policy, in the process placing less emphasis on military instruments and more on economic and diplomatic tools and capabilities. Restoration as a US foreign policy doctrine is about restoring the internal sources of American power and restoring balance to what the United States aims to do in the world and how it does it.

Restoration is not isolationism. As pointed out in the introduction to this book, isolationism is the willful turning away from the world even when a rigorous assessment of a country's national interests (and what could be done to promote them) would argue for acting on their behalf. Isolationism makes no sense in a global world in which the United States cannot wall itself off from the effects of such actual or potential global threats as terrorism, proliferation, protectionism, pandemic disease, climate change, or a loss of access to financial, energy, and mineral resources. Restoration is something very different. Under Restoration, the United States would continue to carry out an active foreign policy: to create or adapt international arrangements to manage the challenges and threats inherent in globalization; to frustrate terrorists; to negotiate bilateral, regional, and global trade, energy, and climate-related pacts; to promote political and economic reform and ameliorate humanitarian crises where and when it makes sense to do so; to invigorate partnerships; and to deal with the threats posed by an aggressive North Korea, a nuclear-armed Iran, and a failing Pakistan. But what distinguishes Restoration first and foremost is its emphasis on rebuilding at home and refocusing abroad, including the limits it would place on what the United States would do with military force on behalf of interests in the Middle East and elsewhere that were less than vital.

Nor should Restoration be understood as a call to abandon the Middle East. The United States retains important and, in some cases, vital interests in that region, including a deep commitment to Israel's security, opposition to the spread of nuclear weapons and to terrorism, and safeguarding access to the region's energy resources. The fact that the United States is moving in the direction of energy self-sufficiency gives it some cushion, but does not alter the fundamental importance of the region. It is essential, though, to acknowledge that between disengagement and preoccupation are myriad policy choices. For more than a decade now, US foreign policy has been both distracted by and distorted by the greater Middle East. Henceforth, direct US military involvement in the region must be scaled back, given competing priorities for American resources of every sort and, in most cases, the likelihood that US efforts to remake societies in this part of the world will fail to justify the investment. In particular, military interventions to overthrow hostile regimes or prop up friendly ones are more and more untenable and should be avoided, because of the certain high costs and low certainty of positive results. More discrete armed action, be it to help maintain the free movement of oil and gas, or to destroy a weapon of mass destruction as it is being developed or readied for use, is a possibility to prepare for. But providing or withholding various forms of diplomatic, economic, intelligence, or military support, be it to influence a country's foreign policy or, in select cases, its domestic trajectory, should constitute the staple of US involvement in this part of the world.

As discussed earlier, prospects for advancing reconciliation and peace between Israel and its neighbors are poor. But this is not an argument for standing pat: Bad situations can and do get worse. Ideally, the Israeli government or the Palestinian Authority or both would put forward a comprehensive peace proposal that would generate real excitement and support both at home and across the divide; failing that, it will probably fall upon the United States to articulate a set of principles that would be at the core of what would be a fair and reasonable peace that would leave all parties better off. Hopefully, a political process and negotiations would ensue. Hamas, which controls Gaza, should be able to participate in negotiations only if it eschews violence and demonstrates a willingness to coexist with Israel. It is anything but clear that Hamas will take these steps; for these and other reasons, the United States should do what it can to bolster the ability of moderate forces in the Palestinian community. The US government should also discourage Israel from those activities, including but not limited to settlement construction, that work against what prospects remain to create a viable Palestinian state.

Implicit in Restoration is a greater focus on the Asia-Pacific, the region that is home to the world's largest and most dynamic economies and the bulk of the world's principal powers, and where the United States has a broad range of interests and commitments. This is largely consistent with the articulation in late 2011 by President Obama of a new strategy in which the United States would pivot from the Middle East to Asia.[1] The idea made sense despite the unfortunate terminology: *Pivot* suggests something much too sharp, both by suggesting too dramatic a pullback from the Middle East and by overlooking all that the United States has done over the decades in the Far East. *Rebalancing* is a better word and, not surprisingly, was later introduced for just that reason. The Obama administration also emphasized more than it might have the military dimensions of the new policy. Of greater importance than the additional deployment of twenty-five hundred marines in Australia is the direction of US diplomacy vis-à-vis China and its neighbors, the availability of economic assistance to promote political and economic development in the region's poorer countries, and the ability to bring into existence a new trade agreement (the Trans-Pacific Partnership, or TPP) quickly and with as many members of the region as possible.

To be sure, the United States has a large stake in Asia's stability, including a number of specific treaty commitments. The best way to assure the region's stability is for the United States to stay active, be a reliable strategic partner, and be present in every sense and sphere, lest other countries either accommodate stronger neighbors or become both more nationalist and aggressive themselves. Thus it continues to make sense for American troops (now numbering twenty-eight thousand) to be stationed in South Korea despite the passage of time and the South's own economic and military strength. The fact that Seoul, the large, modern capital of the Republic of Korea, is located so close to the border with the North makes defense more difficult. Any war would be costly, given this geographic reality and the firepower of the North. Deterring a second Korean War is a high priority. It would help to make clear that any future conflict will end with the unification of the entire peninsula under the South. This should reinforce what restraint exists in North Korea—and reinforce China's willingness to use its influence to rein in Pyongyang, which is more than it admits to, considering North Korea's reliance on China for much of its energy and trade. The United States can also try to reassure China that any unified Korea would be nonnuclear and home to only a small number of US troops, if any. Such reassurance is unlikely to turn Chinese policy around, but it is worth introducing all the same, given the potential for miscalculation and conflict.

If joining in the defense of South Korea would be relatively straightforward, thanks to US treaty commitments, what the United States would do in other conflicts in the region is more ambiguous. The United States has obligations to Taiwan, as well as to Japan, the Philippines, and Australia. American foreign policy faces a delicate balancing act: It must communicate sufficient resolve to its friends and allies, so as not to encourage aggression against them, but not unconditional resolve, lest it potentially lead them to undertake provocative or even reckless behavior. This translates into continuing to provide limited military support of Taiwan, yet at the same time discouraging any unilateral effort on its part to alter the political status quo. It also means close consultations with Japan and the Philippines in particular, so that Chinese assertiveness does not go unmet, but also so that those countries neither say nor do things that would lead to a crisis that could bring the United States and China into direct confrontation.

The rebalancing intrinsic to Restoration would also encompass the Western Hemisphere, and North America in particular. The agenda is filled with issues that bridge foreign and domestic policy alike: energy, trade, investment, infrastructure, water, immigration, homeland security, climate change, drugs, and crime all qualify, as do other issues and subjects. All too often, the agenda has been tackled piecemeal and by mid- or low-ranking officials. What is needed is regular, high-level attention in a comprehensive fashion. The US government should be no less strategic in its approach toward Canada, Mexico, and its other neighbors than it is to other countries and regions critical to its present and future.[2]

Restoration is also entirely consistent with American leadership. I would actually go beyond that; it is a prerequisite for effective American leadership. Only by putting its house in order will the United States have the resources needed to act in the world in a meaningful way, set an example others will be tempted to follow, and signal a latent capacity that will discourage would-be rivals and adversaries from crossing the line. Leadership, just to be clear, is not to be confused with unilateralism, as leadership requires partners if it is to have any meaning. There may be occasions for acting alone, but they will be the exception, especially when the resource costs are great or the nature of the struggle requires widespread participation, which is almost always the case when the challenge is a global one. The specifics of leadership can and should change from situation to situation, depending on the interests at stake, what others are prepared to do, the nature of what is required, and the potential of the United States on its own to do some or all of what is required if the contemplated action is to have the desired effect. Depending on these considerations, leadership can take place from in front, behind, or somewhere in between.

Under Restoration, the United States would operate in the world under a more realistic premise, one based less on the calculation of what it might accomplish (and what it might cost) if everything were to break its way, and more on what might be avoided and what it could cost if things did not. You might call it a less discretionary, less upbeat approach to the world. There would be less resort to military force, especially for the purpose of remaking other societies. There would also be, as a rule of thumb, fewer wars of choice. Wars of choice are defined as armed interventions where either the interests at stake are less than vital or where alternative policies appear to be viable. Recent wars of choice include Vietnam, the second Iraq war, and the recent Libyan intervention.

However, there would certainly continue to be wars of necessity, which involve vital interests where no alternatives exist to using military force or where the alternatives have been tried and failed. Modern wars of necessity include the Korean War, the first Iraq war, and Afghanistan after 9/11. Interestingly, Afghanistan evolved into a costly war of choice when the Obama administration sharply increased force levels and elected to target the Taliban and not just al-Qaeda. Similarly, the Korean War began more than sixty years ago as a war of necessity following the North Korean invasion, but morphed into a war of choice when the United States drove north of the 38th parallel in an effort to reunify the country rather than settling (as it ultimately did, but only after the loss of thirty thousand additional American lives) for liberating South Korea.

There would be no more large-scale military-dominated experiments in remaking other societies on the order of either Iraq or Afghanistan. "Less nation-building abroad, more at home," might be a bumper sticker for Restoration. Training and advising programs would continue on a modest scale; counterterrorism would be carried out by US forces as required. But expensive attempts to remake other societies with US military forces' playing a central role would not occur.

Iran and its nuclear ambitions constitute the most obvious near-term dilemma for Restoration. The United States has a good many reasons for preventing Iran from acquiring nuclear weapons; at the same time, the United States has a strategic interest in avoiding another costly war in the Middle East, something that would be inconsistent with Restoration's twin goals of increased focus on the home front and decreased military involvement in the Middle East. Thus, the bar for initiating a preventive military strike on the Iranian nuclear program would have to be high. It would be a war of choice: Even though US national interests are vital, policies other than using military force exist that could be employed to look after those interests. As a result, and before using or supporting a preventive strike on Iran, the United States should consider the chances it would destroy much of Iran's relevant capacity, the costs of likely retaliation by Iran, the implications for other US interests in the region, the prospects that a nuclear Iran could be confidently deterred, how much confidence there was that the proliferation aspirations of other regional states could be managed though alternative policies, and the impact of such a scenario on the chances for meaningful political change inside Iran once the dust settled. It is possible that all these considerations would be satisfied, but it is a high bar. And it would also be essential to demonstrate beforehand that negotiations with Iran could not produce an acceptable outcome because Iran was unwilling to accept a reasonable compromise.

President Obama appeared to cast his support for a doctrine of Restoration in his June 22, 2011, remarks announcing the beginning of troop reductions in Afghanistan. "America, it is time to focus on nation-building here at home," he said.[3] The decision to bring US troops home from Iraq was arguably consistent with this theme, although so, too, would have been a decision to maintain a small, residual US force in that country.[4] Also compatible with Restoration is the policy of sharply limiting US military involvement in Syria and placing a greater emphasis on the Asia-Pacific. A number of other policies implemented during President Obama's first term were inconsistent, however, including the decision to triple American force levels in Afghanistan, followed by the slow pace of reductions once they were initiated; the decision to intervene directly with military forces in Libya; and the unwillingness to embrace the sort of comprehensive deficit-reduction plan put forward by the Simpson-Bowles Commission in late 2010.

Restoration is, on one level, a national security doctrine for all seasons. At its center is the notion of solvency, the idea that what the United States does abroad should not undermine the fundamental economic health and strength of the country. But on another level, Restoration is a national security doctrine for a particular set of circumstances. Two stand out. Domestic economic and social challenges must be acute, and the international environment must be relatively forgiving; that is, presenting no existential threat. It turns out that precisely these two characteristics capture what the United States faces at home and abroad, today and for some time to come.

How long should Restoration remain the foreign policy of the United States? In one sense it is tempting to say forever, in that solvency is a permanent prerequisite of American strength. But the case for Restoration diminishes as either the domestic foundations of American economic and social strength are shored up or as the international situations evolves, either in the direction of posing a greater threat (which might call for something more akin to containment and greater resource commitment to national security) or greater opportunity (something that would set the stage for a fuller embrace of integration).

A Defensible Defense

The previous section explained that Restoration is in no way to be confused with isolationism; the purpose here is to make clear that Restoration is in no way about disarming. It is about reducing what is spent on defense without jeopardizing national security.

The decisions to scale back American involvement decisively in Iraq and gradually in Afghanistan constitute important first steps. At its peak, US policy toward Iraq and Afghanistan cost close to $200 billion a year, more than 25 percent of total US defense spending.[1] This came to just over 1 percent of GDP. Spending for Iraq is now minimal; spending on Afghanistan is now less than $100 billion and should be well below that by 2014, even if one adds the cost of retaining a modest American troop presence there. The difference between this level of spending and what the United States was devoting to defense operations at the peak of the two wars will free up much-needed dollars for purposes ranging from deficit reduction to domestic investment.

These troop drawdowns will also allow the US military to begin to recover from these two conflicts. Neither soldiers nor equipment can sustain the pace that has been asked of them. Recruitment and retention of highly skilled individuals in the armed forces should increase as the US level of effort in the two conflicts decreases. Some needed military modernization that has been postponed can take place, although this will have to be weighed against alternative (nonmilitary) uses for resources.

US policy could and should go even further: to accelerate the drawdown of its military forces and bring the bulk of them home from Afghanistan by the end of 2013. This proposal will be applauded by some and criticized by others; indeed, it already has had such an effect when I have said or written similar things. The criticism—that what I am calling for is tantamount to "cutting and running," something that makes failure inevitable, diminishes the sacrifices made up to this point, and raises questions of US credibility—is worth mentioning, as the rebuttal makes for a relevant examination of foreign policy.

Success in Afghanistan is beyond reach, if by *success* is meant bringing about an Afghanistan that is on a long-term path of stability, prosperity, and democracy. I would also argue that the United States does not have a vital interest in accomplishing all this; US interests in Afghanistan (such as promoting a more tolerant Afghan society) are real but less than vital, as well as difficult to act on. What the United States *is* in a position to do is tied to its ensuring that Afghanistan does not again become a launching pad for terrorism-related events on the scale of 9/11.

Second, it is irresponsible to continue to commit resources, and above all to send US forces into harm's way, on behalf of a policy that doesn't warrant their sacrifice either because the interests are not sufficiently important or the prospects for succeeding are not sufficiently good. Lasting success is beyond reach, given the nature of Afghanistan's government and society, the zeal of the Taliban, and Pakistan's continued willingness to provide sanctuary for the Taliban and other groups determined to shoot their way to power. Admitting and acting on this judgment in no way takes away from all that was committed and sacrificed up to now: Sometimes an undertaking is worth trying and doing because it is impossible to know with certainty in advance what can be accomplished at what cost. But policy must be revisited and revised once the answers to such questions are available.

A related argument put forward for "staying the course" in Afghanistan is that instability there would exacerbate instability in Pakistan, a country where the United States has more important national interests: the presence of the world's most dangerous terrorists, a robust nuclear weapons program, and a population five times that of Afghanistan. While this may be true, it is hard to be more concerned about Pakistan's stake in Afghan stability than Pakistan's government, which is actively supporting the very forces that are working to undermine Afghanistan. And while a weak and unstable Afghanistan could become something of a launching pad for radicals who seek to destabilize Pakistan, it should be pointed out that such radicals are already able to operate relatively freely from within Pakistan itself. All of which to say is that Afghanistan is far down the list of factors that will determine Pakistan's future stability or orientation.

Changing policy course is never without risks. A great power that wants to remain one should be wary of compromising its reputation for staying power. Credibility and reliability matter. But a large sustained effort tends to settle the point; Afghanistan is already the longest war in American history. It is difficult to argue the United States failed to do enough on behalf of that country or to do it long enough.

The critics of reducing or concluding a military commitment also tend to exaggerate the adverse consequences of doing so.

The consequences of the US withdrawal from South Vietnam (resisted by the Nixon and Ford administrations but imposed by Congress) look different and far better today than were widely predicted at the time. The United States is central to the region's future and has good or good enough ties with a unified Vietnam, China, and traditional American allies. Similar things could be said for what ensued after the decision by Ronald Reagan to withdraw all US forces from Lebanon in 1984. US influence in the region hardly disappeared; less than a decade later, the United States put together the unprecedented international coalition that ousted Iraq from Kuwait, and then followed up this military victory with the diplomatic breakthrough that was the Madrid peace conference, which for the first time in history brought together representatives of Israel and Arab governments face to face to negotiate peace. Even when it suffers setbacks or defeats, the United States retains enormous ability to shape events around the world.

Savings on what is spent on behalf of national security need not and should not be limited to savings derived from winding down the two wars. Core defense spending, without the additional costs associated with Afghanistan, comes to slightly more than $500 billion a year, more than China, Russia, Japan, India, and the EU combined. Could more be spent? Of course—but US interests and the threats to them do not warrant spending more. In addition, spending somewhat less on defense makes it easier to move the US budget toward balance, something that provides a basis for long-term national security, including more defense spending if need be.

Could more be cut? Again, the answer is yes, but in this case one should ask, "At what risk?" The pattern in history is to cut back too much after times of great exertion. What should matter (in addition to domestic requirements for resources) are strategic projections; that is, where US interests may be coming under pressure or attack and where this country must be able to respond. The United States needs to be prepared to act against Iran's nuclear program, help defend South Korea from its northern neighbor, carry out limited counterterrorist and humanitarian actions, and provide reassurance to its allies in Asia. As this list suggests, there is always the possibility of simultaneous contingencies.[2] Given the inherent uncertainty associated with this era of history, ensuring that US forces and national security resources across the board are both flexible and adaptable to engage in multiple regions of the world makes a great deal of sense. One could do worse here than keep in mind the words of Robert Gates: "Our record since Vietnam of predicting where we would use military force 6 months or 12 months from now is perfect. We have never, ever gotten it right once. So we live in that kind of an unpredictable world, and therefore to structure our forces against one or another particular potential adversary I think would be a grave mistake."[3]

As is always the case, what matters more than how much is spent on defense (or any policy, for that matter) is how it is spent. Avoiding large-scale land wars and large humanitarian interventions allows for reductions in the size of both the army and marines. The one foreseeable large land war of necessity would be on the Korean Peninsula. (An Iran conflict would likely involve mostly air and naval forces.) Greater emphasis on Asia and the Pacific argues for selective increases in air force and navy funding, although some of the most expensive weapons systems meant for conventional warfare should be cut back in light of existing capabilities and relative American advantages over imaginable foes. Research and development should continue to be a priority as a hedge against future uncertainty and as a means to ensure the United States is in a position to exploit the latest new technologies. Reform of the military entitlements system (retirement and health plans are consuming an ever larger and unsustainable share of the total defense budget) and a reduction in the size of the nuclear arsenal (which is still larger than post–Cold War realities would dictate) would help reduce the need for tradeoffs within the defense budget. All things considered, a strong case can be made for defense spending at a level somewhat below the current one. Core defense spending that was reduced by 5 to 10 percent or some $25 to $50 billion would more than adequately cover existing needs and make it less difficult for the US government to move in the direction of solvency.[4]

Funds allocated to other national security functions—foreign assistance, diplomacy, intelligence, and homeland security—should not be immune from scrutiny and, where warranted on the merits or because of overall fiscal considerations, from cuts. That said, they are relatively modest in scale and for the most part good value, considering the benefits that accrue from them. Foreign aid, in particular, is a far smaller budgetary item than many Americans imagine. So, too, is the cost of diplomacy. These other national security activities add just over $150 billion a year; combined national security spending (minus the costs of the Afghanistan operation) thus comes to about $650 or $700 billion a year and around $750 to $800 billion including it. This is less than 20 percent of federal spending and only some 4 percent of GDP. This is both affordable and consistent with a doctrine of Restoration.

It is equally important to recognize that no amount of savings on defense and national security could fix what ails the American economy. Even the most aggressive reductions imaginable—say, to cut core defense spending by 20 percent or roughly $100 billion a year—would have at most a modest impact on the deficit. Against this Americans must consider

Part III

Restoration at Home

Restoration is not just about doing less or acting more discriminately abroad; to the contrary, it is even more about doing the right things at home. The principal focus is on restoring the economic, social, and physical foundations of American power. A decade of adopting and living according to a doctrine of Restoration would help the United States shore up the economic foundations of its traditional strengths for decades to come. As has been argued here, cutting back on national security spending and wars of choice could not accomplish this on their own, but doing so would constitute one component of moving toward fiscal balance. A policy along these lines would allow the United States to deal with near-term threats or challenges, should they arise. It would also put the country back in a position to lead by example; one of the most important foreign policy strengths this country possesses is the demonstrated success of its economy and political system. Both are now tarnished, a reality that makes others much less likely to adopt open economic and political models and instead opt for more statist systems with less scope for individual freedom and markets.

To speak of the domestic challenge facing the United States is, in reality, to speak of multiple challenges. The list is virtually endless and no doubt highly subjective, but I would highlight five core elements: reducing the federal deficit and the ratio of national debt to GDP, putting into place a comprehensive energy strategy, improving the quality of education, upgrading the country's physical infrastructure, and modernizing an out-of-date immigration policy. Doing all this, in addition to adopting some specific economic reforms, would allow the United States to restore its economic growth to levels closer to those that have characterized much of the post–World War II era but that have been out of reach over recent years.

Such levels of federal debt are unsustainable. The situation gets even worse if state and local debt, as well as the enormous debt (an estimated $12 trillion) of so-called Government Sponsored Enterprises, such as Fannie Mae and Freddie Mac, are added in.[2] Just financing all this debt threatens to absorb a significant percentage of the funds that would otherwise be available for education, research, and infrastructure: Increasingly, the United States will be forced to eat its seed corn to pay for its past and present. American ability to compete successfully in an increasingly competitive global economy will suffer. It was Herb Stein, one of Richard Nixon's principal economic advisers, who observed that things that cannot go on forever will end. Well, this will end. It is a question of how. And if nothing is done, it will also become a question of when the world will grow weary and wary of lending more dollars to the United States, and will demand higher returns for so doing. The danger is twofold: At a minimum, it will force the Federal Reserve to raise interest rates, in the process dampening economic growth that is already well below historic averages; at worst, it will happen suddenly, forcing draconian and ill-considered cuts in what America spends.

The United States is fast approaching one of those truly historic turning points: Either it will act to get its fiscal house in order, thereby restoring the prerequisites of this country's primacy, or it will fail to and, as a result, suffer both the domestic and international consequences. The world is looking for a signal that the United States has the political will and ability to make hard choices. Eliminating the deficit is not necessary, but it does need to be reduced to a degree considerably larger than what was required to avoid going over the so-called fiscal cliff. The goal should be to reduce this country's deficit by some $250 billion per year over the next four to five years, or until the budget is balanced but for interest payments on the debt. This can be accomplished responsibly and gradually, without in the process throwing the United States back into recession. If this is accomplished, it will contribute to economic growth, which in turn will reduce the ratio of debt to GDP, in the process sending just the signal the world is looking for.

The United States being at such a juncture is not totally unexpected, in that other great powers throughout history have seen their circumstances reduced. But imperial overstretch is not the real issue here. The combined cost of the Iraq and Afghan wars during their peak years accounted for 10 to 15 percent of the annual deficit and are responsible for much less than that of the cumulative debt. The principal reasons for questioning the Iraq war several years ago and Afghanistan now are strategic more than economic. This leads to the larger point. Fiscal, economic, and political failures at home are placing at risk the continued ability of the United States to exert the global influence that it could and should have. Ill-advised American activity in the world is not what jeopardizes American solvency; rather, American profligacy at home threatens American power and security. Yet at their great peril, the American people and their elected representatives postpone addressing the country's debt addiction.

Bringing the budget into primary balance (paying for everything except interest on the debt) requires that four different but related components be addressed: discretionary domestic spending, defense and national security, entitlements, and taxes. Defense has already been addressed; core defense spending can be reduced to slightly below $500 billion a year without jeopardizing American security. But no amount of defense or, more broadly, national security spending cuts can bring the budget into anything approaching balance. This can only come from reductions in entitlements and domestic spending, and what is raised through taxation. (A final area of spending is mandatory as it involves paying off what was borrowed. Doing so currently consumes some 6 percent of federal spending. But here the objective is to limit this amount both by slowing the accumulation of new debt and by doing nothing that would increase the rates at which money was borrowed. This means avoiding any rekindling of inflation and not raising questions about the ability of the United States to be good for what it owes.)

Federal spending outside national security and interest payments is a mix of mandatory and discretionary spending that covers a wide range of traditional domestic functions, including health, retirement, welfare and other programs that form the so-called safety net, infrastructure, transportation, education, agricultural subsidies, and a good deal else. Some of this qualifies as investment, some as support. One way to think about the US budget (now just under $4 trillion a year, or some 23 percent of GDP) is one-fifth each national security, health (mostly Medicare and Medicaid), retirement (mostly Social Security), some 12 percent additional safety net (welfare, unemployment and disability payments), and 6 percent interest on the debt—leaving just 20 percent, or some $750 billion a year, for all else. Projected cuts to this category over the coming decade that were included in the 2011 Budget Control Act surely should be made, but the "all else" is simply not large enough to contribute all that much to deficit reduction, even if you wanted to, which in the cases of investment in human and physical capital, you would not.

The best way to move the budget in the direction of balance is through a mix of spending cuts and higher revenues; in other words, selective tax increases. A ratio on the order of three to one—$3 dollars in spending cuts for every dollar in tax increases—holds out the best way of getting from here to there without shutting down investment or hampering growth. But this can only be done intelligently if spending on entitlements— Social Security and, above all, health care—is brought under control. The trajectory of Social Security spending can be reined in through a mix of gradually increasing the retirement or eligibility age, means-testing payments so that the wealthiest either receive smaller payments or pay higher taxes on them, selectively reducing the fast-growing area of disability payments, and altering the formula by which annual payments are adjusted for inflation so that the increases are more in line with the increases in prices of what seniors actually tend to buy. One could also raise the cap on payroll tax deductions that fund the program.[3]

Health care is far more important as a source of deficits. Willie Sutton robbed banks because that was where the money was; anyone wanting to tame the US budget must address health care because that will increasingly be the source of the deficit. The statistics are stark. The United States spends nearly a fifth of its total GDP on health care, nearly twice the average of other advanced economies.[4] Alas, outcomes are no better for it. This is because of unnecessary testing and procedures (the system is geared to what is performed rather than results), inadequate focus on preventive health, and an emphasis on prolonging life in situations where there is little reason to believe treatment will improve health. Unlike Social Security, however, there is no straightforward path to improving matters, with some favoring a larger role for government and advisory bodies that would establish guidelines for treatment, others on vouchers and market forces. That said, significant savings could be realized from raising the age for Medicare eligibility, requiring increased co-payments, limiting malpractice torts, means-testing, and introducing a host of administrative reforms that would introduce best practices to a larger number of providers.

Taxes form the last piece of the puzzle. As is the case with spending, the composition of taxes matters as much or more than levels. The American Taxpayer Relief Act of 2012, which averted the so-called fiscal cliff and was signed into law in

January 2013, raised marginal income tax levels on the wealthiest Americans, increased rates for both capital gains and dividend income, placed limits on certain itemized deductions for those in the higher tax brackets, and slightly elevated the tax rate for estates over $5 million. Payroll tax rates went back up to previous levels. Additional revenues could come from further tweaking of rates and deductions, eliminating some remaining exceptions or subsidies, and faster growth. One could also adopt a modest consumption or value added tax (VAT), something that would raise revenue and encourage savings.[5]

All told, the fiscal cliff deal will raise approximately $600 billion in additional revenue over the next ten years. A realistic analysis of the discretionary spending cuts in the 2011 Budget Control Act suggests that they will save about $1.5 trillion over the same period. Together, the two bills will reduce the deficit by about $2 trillion over the next decade—about half of what is needed to achieve the $4 trillion in deficit reduction most analysts believe is necessary to put America back on stable financial footing. Much of the remaining savings will need to come from entitlements. The National Commission on Fiscal Responsibility and Reform, a bipartisan group created by President Obama in 2010 and commonly known as the Simpson-Bowles Commission after its chairmen, retired senator Alan Simpson and former White House chief of staff Erskine Bowles, suggested a comprehensive plan designed to slash the debt by $4 trillion over ten years through a mixture of cuts in both domestic spending and national security, selective tax increases, and Medicare reforms.[6] One can quibble with the details, but something like it is called for if the United States is to have the resources it will need to shield itself from the pressures of markets or unfriendly central banks and present a model of political and economic competence that the world will want to emulate.

Energy

Energy, and in particular oil and gas, is central to the function of modern economies, for transportation as well as for home heating, farming, and manufacturing. There are many other energy sources, including nuclear, coal, and various renewables—hydroelectric, wind, solar, and so forth—but for the foreseeable future these cannot take the place of oil and gas.

Oil is of particular significance. The sale of oil in large quantities at relatively high prices has massively enriched several countries with otherwise poor economies, including Russia, Saudi Arabia, Iran, Iraq, Venezuela, and Nigeria, a transfer that has enabled them to spend a great deal on arms and maintain political order at home through government largesse. Those consuming their oil, such as the United States, are vulnerable to interruptions of supply and increases in price.

The fact that oil is so important has had an enormous impact on US foreign policy.[1] The United States did not fight multiple wars in the Middle East so as to gain access to oil supplies for the benefit of commercial interests, but it did in part fight those wars to ensure that a strategic commodity would not be controlled by individuals or regimes hostile to US interests.

The need to import large amounts of oil has also added to the budget deficit, weakened the dollar, and contributed to US economic vulnerability. And on top of all this is the reality that the burning of fossil fuels, including oil, has contributed significantly to climate change.

Many of these trends can be traced back forty years, to the first oil shock at the time of the 1973 Middle East conflict. Some four decades later, the United States, which possesses only 2 percent of the world's proved reserves of oil, produces some 12 percent of world output—approximately 10 million barrels a day. The problem is that the United States consumes 19 million barrels of oil a day, nearly twice what it produces. The difference between what is produced domestically and what is consumed is made up by imports.

However, some aspects of America's energy situation are strongly positive. US oil production, which was falling for decades, has actually risen in recent years, thanks in large part to new technology that makes it possible to find and produce oil that only a few years ago would have remained beneath the surface. This trend is expected to continue. The International Energy Agency now projects that the United States will overtake Saudi Arabia and become the world's largest oil producer by 2020.[2] At the same time, US consumption of oil is about what it was a decade ago, even though the economy has become much larger; what this shows is that the link between energy use and economic output (energy intensity) is less than it was prior to the introduction of new efficiencies.

Welcome, too, is the evolving nature of US oil dependence. The single largest source of oil for the United States is North America. Canada alone provides one-fourth of all American oil imports. (This is one reason the proposed oil pipeline extension linking Canada and the United States should be built.) Mexico is the second largest. Only one-fifth of US oil imports (equaling 10 percent of American consumption) comes from the Middle East. This positive pattern of diversifying overseas sources of oil leaves the United States less vulnerable to supply shortages caused by conditions within or the policies of a particular producing country. Overall, US imports now account for less than half the oil consumed in this country. In short, the trends are all good: Domestic production is up, consumption is down, imports are down.

The best news of all concerns natural gas. The United States is now the world's largest producer. What is more, proved reserves of natural gas in this country are increasing because of technological innovations that make it possible to identify and tap enormous gas deposits in shale formations. Natural gas can be substituted for other forms of energy in many areas; it is both plentiful in the United States and, when burned, contributes less than oil and far less than coal to climate change.

But all this good news should not generate complacency. The now-realistic possibility of achieving a status close to energy self-sufficiency, in which American energy is either produced domestically or imported from Canada and Mexico, is not the same as energy independence. The United States cannot insulate itself from the global energy market. It will be directly and indirectly affected by shortages of supplies and increases in oil prices brought on by either long-term trends (e.g., much-increased demand for oil in China and India) or crisis (e.g., a war with Iran or instability in Saudi Arabia or Nigeria). The United States will be similarly affected if the economies of those countries it trades with suffer energy shortages and higher prices. This, too, is an unavoidable dimension of interdependence and globalization.

The United States needs to be made more energy resilient and energy responsible alike. The objective should be to ensure that energy use decreases as a fraction of GDP, that US direct dependence on the Middle East for oil continues to diminish, and that coal constitutes a reduced component of America's energy profile. Such an approach would reduce what this country spends on energy, its vulnerability to instability in the Middle East, the upward pressure on oil prices (one result of which is the enriching of Iran), and the American "contribution" to climate change.

A strategy to accomplish this would have a number of components. One commitment should be to continue to expand the domestic production of both oil and gas. Another should be greater coordination with Canada, Mexico, and other Western Hemisphere producers. Regulation of natural gas cannot become so extensive that meaningful production is precluded. Steps should also continue to be made to reduce consumption of oil and, even more important, coal. This requires additional legislation or regulation to mandate greater fuel efficiency for motor vehicles and appliances. An agreement reached in 2011 between the Obama administration and thirteen major car manufacturers to increase fuel economy for cars and light trucks to an average of 54.5 miles per gallon by 2025 was a major step in the right direction.[3] Indeed, it is no exaggeration to point to this measure as one of the major national security achievements of recent years. Natural gas could be substituted for oil for this country's large trucks, a switch that could significantly reduce demand for oil.[4] There should also be an increase in the federal tax on gasoline, which has nominally stayed the same for two decades (slightly more than eighteen cents a gallon), although in reality it is much lower when the effects of inflation are taken into consideration.[5] One idea would be to index the gasoline tax to inflation so that it automatically goes up a small amount each year. Proceeds could be dedicated to rebuilding this country's roads and other forms of infrastructure. A broader tax on carbon could also raise needed revenues, encourage energy efficiency, and enable the United States to take the lead in forging regional and global pacts designed to slow climate change in a manner that did not constrain economic growth.

Any US energy strategy also must encompass nuclear energy. It is a potential problem, not because there is too much of it, but because there is too little. Nuclear plants provide one-fifth of America's electricity. But because of local political pressures, it has been more than forty years since a new nuclear plant was given the go-ahead (and some seventeen years since it first became operational) in the United States.[6] The result is that, for safety reasons, all 103 US nuclear plants will have to be replaced or taken out of operation by midcentury or soon after. Replacing them requires that an average of two new plants per year be built between now and then.[7] This is not happening. So the energy they currently produce will have to be replaced by coal or by using more oil and gas with obvious adverse consequences for climate, national security, or both. Safety concerns (for obvious reasons paramount, given Japan's recent experience) can be mitigated by intelligent siting of new plants, new construction techniques, and improved measures as regards operations and waste disposal and management. Risk cannot be eliminated, but needs to be judged against the costs and risks of using alternative fuels (which contribute to climate change) or strengthening the hands of hostile governments. This argues for ensuring that nuclear energy continues to provide a meaningful share of American electricity well into the future.

Education

Economic performance and competitiveness are based upon many factors, from physical capital to regulatory policy, but no single factor may be as important as education. Education is the mechanism by which we invest in ourselves and in our own collective future.

There is no other way to say it except bluntly: American education at the K–12 level is failing. In recent international tests, American students ranked 13th in reading, 18th in science, and 28th in math.[1] Just one-third of elementary school students in this country are competent in reading and math.[2] The problem is not just those who do not graduate high school; it is that many of those who do (roughly 40 percent) are not prepared for college and require considerable remedial assistance.[3]

This poor K–12 record is also having an impact on American higher education, long an area of comparative advantage for the United States. This country is number one in the world when it comes to a percentage of those between the ages of 55 to 64 with a college degree. But the US ranking falls to tenth place if what is measured are those between the ages of 25 and 34 who hold college degrees. This trend bodes poorly for the future.

There are obvious economic consequences of such numbers; highly skilled workers are an essential component of national competitiveness. Corporations have to locate plants where they have access to such workers, which often translates to locating such facilities outside the United States, a trend reinforced by US immigration and corporate taxation policies. More generally, there is a clear correlation between educational attainment and income; individuals as well as the country are less well off because of the lost productivity resulting from insufficient education.

But the consequences of poor K–12 schooling go beyond the economic. A recent Council on Foreign Relations–sponsored task force warned that this situation jeopardizes America's national cohesion and security alike. "Too many US public schools have stopped teaching civics and citizenship—leaving students without knowledge of their own national history, traditions, and values. Schools have also largely failed to help students become aware of other cultures or the world." The result is a shortage of young men and women who can compete successfully in a global marketplace, serve in the military (among recent high school graduates who are eligible to apply, 30 percent score too low on aptitude tests to be recruited), and in a position to fulfill their obligations to society.

Why is American doing so poorly here? The answer is not for a lack of trying, or at least spending. But in education, as with so much else, there is no direct correlation between spending and results. What matters most is how money is allocated, not how much. The United States spends a great deal on education, more per pupil on primary and secondary education than most countries in the OECD. In total, it spent more than $600 billion on education in 2010; per-pupil costs have more than doubled since 1992, to over $10,000.[4] Yet South

Korea, which scored higher than the United States in all PISA (Programme for International Student Assessment) categories, spends roughly half as much per student. Sweden and Finland spend about a third and a fifth less, respectively, and both scored well above the United States on PISA.[5] What makes it all even more frustrating is that other parts of the American educational system are literally world class. The most promising young people from around the world go to extraordinary lengths to come to the United States to attend its colleges and universities; to the best of my knowledge, few people ever come to this country from abroad to attend a public elementary or high school.

There are many explanations for why K–12 education is so flawed. The quality of teachers turns out to be the most important influence on the quality of education. Unfortunately, and notwithstanding important exceptions, the best and brightest of American society are not making teaching a career. Changing this will require paying the best teachers more and investing more in making teachers better. This can only be accomplished under current and foreseeable budgetary constraints by changing how teacher compensation is determined and moving toward performance as a critical criterion for determining pay, instead of an educator's time in service or number of degrees. Achieving progress will also require a better distribution of employment and compensation within the education establishment; too many resources currently go to administration and other areas that have little or nothing to do with teaching. A longer school year is also a must; the existing academic year may have made sense when most families were agricultural and needed their children to perform farm labor, but it hardly applies now. The Rand Corporation found that the average student loses the equivalent of a month of learning in math and science over the summer; disadvantaged children lose two. And a widely cited Johns Hopkins paper found that summer learning loss could explain about two-thirds of the achievement gap between low- and high-income ninth graders in Baltimore.[6] Greater competition and choice among schools can only help. What is taught and how to test for it also needs to be rethought. The setting of national (Common Core) standards in literacy, math, and science, coupled with financial incentives for schools to adopt them, are a step in the right direction; it would be good if civics were added to this list.[7] In addition, and as many observers have pointed out, the relationship between homework and the classroom needs to "flip"; increasingly, the student can access quality information outside the classroom from a large number of sources, whereas the classroom becomes the place for interaction and discussion. Teachers become less the source of information and more facilitators who monitor students and intervene to enhance learning and understanding.

Last, Americans as a society will also need to recast how they think about education. The current approach is that education is something done near exclusively with, for, and to children and young people in their teens and twenties. Far too much of the US educational system is predicated on what can best be described as the "fill 'er up" model. People go to high school and maybe college, and then are discharged down the highway of life on that one intellectual tank of gas, with little encouragement or assistance to ever stop and refuel thereafter. But it is inconceivable that an eighteen- or twenty-two-year-old has learned by the time he or she graduates what will be enough to make that person a viable, attractive employee twenty years later, when he or she turns forty, much less in forty years, when he or she turns sixty and is still facing as many as ten to twenty years of work. The world, from technology to so much else, is changing too fast for a front-loaded educational approach to make any sense.

Reinforcing this last point is the change in US unemployment. As of this writing, some 40 percent of America's unemployed, or 5 million adults, have been unemployed for more
than six months.[8] With every day that passes, the mismatch
between the skills of the individual and the needs of the work-
place is likely to grow. This gap poses a threat not just to these
individuals but to American economic growth and social cohesion.[9] Making it all the more frustrating is that hundreds of
thousands of jobs are going begging, unfilled because employers
cannot find qualified individuals. The scale of this problem can
be reduced only by making additional education available, most
likely tied to the specific opportunity or industry at hand.[10]

So the country needs to embrace more of what I like to call
the "top 'er off" model of education. What anyone learned in
school would be the foundation, but it would be assumed that
on many occasions he or she would need to learn new skills. If
anything, the pace of change is accelerating; it stands to reason
that the pace of education must keep up. Additional education might require going back to school for a spell, might be
provided by the employer, or might be possible to learn online.
The tax system could create incentives of different sorts, from
deductions for certain types of educational activities, to tax-
advantaged accounts to corporate tax breaks for the training
and then hiring of workers. But whatever the approach or blend
of approaches, a clear need exists to make lifelong learning easy
and attractive.

Infrastructure

This country's engineers grade US infrastructure—America's roads, bridges, transit, rail, aviation, power grid, drinking water, wastewater, and dams—somewhere between C at best and D at worst.[1] This may not technically count as failing, but it comes too close for comfort and is clearly far from what is needed.

The reason is simple: America's infrastructure is starved for cash. The United States is not doing nearly enough to maintain its existing infrastructure (much of which is outdated to begin with), much less modernize and improve it. General tax revenues are too stretched; infrastructure must compete with everything else government does or wants to do at the federal, state, and local level, and often comes up short. And dedicated tax revenues have not come close to keeping pace with needs. The federal gasoline tax, the principal mechanism for funding the country's roads, has been kept steady at 18.4 cents for twenty years now.[2] The result is that the Federal Highway Trust Fund now spends considerably more than it takes in.

The direct costs of substandard infrastructure are large and growing. Estimates are just that, but inadequate infrastructure contributes to accidents (which increase health-care costs and keep workers out of work), wastes precious time (hours spent in traffic jams, on slow trains, sitting on runways because airports cannot handle the flow of planes, goods backed up in ports), jeopardizes health, and squanders energy. At worst, we have seen in extreme conditions—such as in New Orleans and its surrounding areas after Hurricane Katrina and in New York and New Jersey after Hurricane Sandy—how inadequate infrastructure can bring entire cities and regions to a halt.

Continuing down this road (so to speak) will have measurable effects, and I am not just talking about more potholes. By 2020, crumbling infrastructure could shave as much as a full percentage point off the country's growth—a staggering amount, when you consider that the economy averaged only 2 percent annual growth during the first decade of this century.[3] Americans waste more than 4 billion hours a year stuck in traffic on congested roads, costing nearly $80 billion a year in wasted time and gas. Nearly a third of all miles driven in America are driven in traffic; in urban areas, it is 40 percent. Car crashes, often attributed to poor road maintenance, "cost the US $230 billion per year—$819 for each resident in medical costs, lost productivity, travel delays, workplace costs, insurance costs, and legal costs," according to the American Society of Civil Engineers.[4]

What makes things worse is that the United States is not operating in a vacuum here. While American infrastructure is being allowed to deteriorate, other countries are not standing still. Ten years ago, US infrastructure ranked fifth in the world in terms of quality. A decade later, it ranks twenty-fourth, passed by the likes of Barbados, Malaysia, and Oman. The United States spends less than 2 percent of its GDP on infrastructure, whereas China spends closer to 9 percent; and India, 8 percent.[5] This is an investment in the future. The impact on competitiveness will only grow with the passage of time.

There is a national security angle as well. We have to assume that the future will include disasters both natural (e.g., hurricanes, floods, earthquakes) and man-made (e.g., terrorism). Prevention and protection will not always work. When disaster occurs, it is essential that the country as a whole and at the city and state level have the capacity to limit the effects and recover with as little loss of life and economic disruption as possible. A robust and in some instances redundant infrastructure is a critical component of such resilience.

As is almost always the case, there are many things the United States can and should do. Raising the federal gasoline tax would help. Indeed, this would help many times over: it would generate much-needed revenue for highway and bridge repair and expansion, reduce consumption of oil, and result in the release of less carbon into the atmosphere. I appreciate the difficult politics of doing this, but, and as suggested earlier, indexing the tax to inflation would be relatively painless and make a meaningful difference over time.

Many other remedies warrant consideration and in many cases adoption, some aimed at limiting demand. These include so-called congestion pricing (fees imposed on certain days and at certain times to discourage travel in crowded areas at the most crowded times) and user fees (tolls for roads, bridges, and tunnels). New sources of funding are decidedly necessary, given that government resources are already overstretched. Public-private partnerships such as a local or national infrastructure banks could seed and coordinate projects, with the bulk of the resources coming from the private sector (including from overseas investors) and paid back over time by user fees. Such private-sector mechanisms are essential, as there is no way governments at any level will be able to come up with sufficient dollars to fund even a modest portion of what is required.

There is one other reason to head down this path. Improving infrastructure would not only boost American economic growth, improve public safety, and increase this country's competitiveness, it would provide employment for those working on the projects and living near them. It is rare in the public policy arena that one encounters win-win propositions, but rebuilding this country's infrastructure has the potential to be one of them.

incentives to come here illegally, such as by making would-be employers liable for civil and criminal penalties. Recent numbers suggest US policy is largely working, in part because illegal entry has become more difficult, in part because the absence of jobs in the United States (and their relative abundance in Mexico, which is enjoying a higher rate of growth than the United States) has dramatically reduced the incentive of people looking for work to try to come to this country.[3] Smaller families in Mexico are also reducing the number of potential immigrants. The immigration problem could soon be one of too few and not too many people coming from south of the border.

The second dimension and increasingly the most difficult to resolve is the status of the 11 million or so men, women, and children in this country who have arrived or remained illegally. The option of forcing them to leave does not pass the serious test. The real question is whether they are forced to linger in their current situation or allowed to travel along a path that would result in normalization and legalization of their status, be it as full citizens or something else. The argument against establishing such a path is that it would penalize those waiting patiently to enter legally and that it would create a precedent that might encourage even more people to enter or stay illegally in the hope that one day they, too, will be forgiven. (This is a version of what economists call moral hazard.) Against these concerns are the arguments that current policy is forcing some 11 million people to live in the shadows, limiting what they can contribute to this country. There are both humanitarian and economic reasons for normalizing the situations of most of these people using criteria that favor those with education, who have an employment record, have met tax obligations, who have performed national service, and have no criminal record.[4] Requiring that individuals meet these tests, and making sure

Immigration Act of 1990. Temporary increases in the number of H-1B visas introduced in 1999 and 2000 were allowed to lapse.[6]

The number of green cards and visas does not come even close to meeting the demand for workers with advanced degrees and special skills. One result is that companies (Microsoft but one of many) have elected to build facilities in Canada and elsewhere because they cannot hire the number of qualified workers they need. (This also reflects problems in American education, as discussed earlier.) A more general consequence of its immigration laws is that the United States is less competitive than it ought to be. There is a real connection between immigrants and both entrepreneurship and innovation. The 2010 US Census found that 5.1 percent of naturalized citizens were employed in their own businesses, compared with 3.7 percent of native-born Americans. In Massachusetts, immigrants make up only 14 percent the state's population, but founded 61 percent of its new businesses in 2008. A 2011 report by the Partnership for a New American Economy found that immigrant entrepreneurs established nearly 20 percent of all Fortune 500 companies, generating $1.7 trillion in annual revenue and employing nearly 4 million people worldwide. A separate study found that, between 1995 and 2005, 25 percent of new technology and engineering companies were founded or cofounded by foreign-born entrepreneurs, creating 450,000 jobs. In 2006, immigrants received 40 percent of US science and engineering PhDs and 60 percent of the computer science ones. Sixty percent of postdoctoral researchers in these fields are foreign born. More than half the recent labor force growth in this country has been fueled by immigration, allowing the United States largely to avoid the working population declines seen in Japan and Europe.[7]

American lawmakers and interest groups may be oblivious to such a correlation, but other governments are not. Canada,

Australia, and the United Kingdom have introduced an immigration policy based on the attributes of applicants; points are awarded for education and skills and the like, and those who score sufficiently high are admitted. The caps on its ability to accept such people thus hits the United States twice: It denies itself the best talent, in the process making its workforce less competitive, but channels workers with these advantages to others, making its competitors better.

Something similar to a rating system should be considered. The number and mix of visas could be determined annually to reflect market needs. Or numbers could simply be increased with businesses allowed to sponsor more individuals. Either way, green cards should be increased for those with needed skills; so, too, should H-1B visas. Simply going back to pre-9/11 levels of H-1B visas (about twice the current rate) would be a step in the right direction. More generally, the basis of US immigration policy needs to evolve, from one of principally family-related concerns to one in which economic criteria have at least equal weight. Immigration needs to be seen for what it is: as an opportunity as much as a problem, and as a strategic instrument. Ideally, the United States would adopt comprehensive immigration reform, to deal with border security, to create a path to legal status or citizenship for the 11 million people already here but living outside the law, and legal immigration, attracting to its shores foreign workers with the education and skills to keep American businesses competitive.

This leads to an area in which education and immigration policies come together because of the failings of each: Despite the fact that the unemployment rate hovers around 8 percent, and despite the fact that millions of Americans are out of work, hundreds of thousands of private sector jobs are going unfilled. One reason is that they require skills missing from the American work force. The United States needs either to improve its educational system so that the unemployed or new workers come to possess those skills—something that will take years or decades if it is in fact willing and able to do it, or to increase opportunities for foreign workers with such skills (many of which were acquired while they were students at American colleges and universities) to come and live and work and stay in this country—or both.

Economic Growth

In some ways the most fundamental task facing the United States is to restore historical levels of economic growth. Growth averaged 3.3 percent for fifty years, from 1960 to 2010, but is currently running at half that. A return to relatively high rates of growth is essential if this country is to maintain is social cohesion and to have the resources and the outlook it will need to lead the world and provide for its citizens.

Why has US economic growth slowed? Some of the reasons are structural, in that they are linked to fundamental changes in the economic environment. Here I would list technological change, which in many instances has made certain jobs redundant, along with globalization and the growing competition from others who can produce goods of equal quality at a lower cost. At the same time, some of the reasons for the slowdown are more cyclical, the result of specific circumstances, such as the 2008 financial crisis.

The consequences of prolonged low growth (and the continued stagnation or, in many cases, fall in the incomes of many American households) would be serious and potentially dire. Fewer resources could be tapped for international involvement;

the US role in the world would necessarily be more limited than interests and conditions would warrant. The American public would become more preoccupied with national rather than international challenges. Friends and foes alike would have to recalculate based on what the United States could be expected to do. The appeal of the US political and economic model would also be distinctly limited. The net result would be a world less peaceful, less free, and less prosperous. Prolonged low growth would also affect the full range of services and the quality of life within the country; if growth were sufficiently low for an extended period, it would threaten the very fabric of American society.

Sustained higher growth will only come about if a number of factors discussed here line up: much greater budgetary discipline, a smart energy policy, improved K–12 education, modernized infrastructure, and increased strategic immigration.[1] There is a potential virtuous cycle here: Investing in the prerequisites of growth will increase growth, which in turn will generate more resources for investing in activities that will generate growth. To the list of prerequisites must be added particular policies able to accelerate economic growth. Reducing regulations that on review are too costly or put US firms at a competitive disadvantage also qualifies. There is a danger in going too far—what was allowed to evolve in the way of home mortgages is a case in point, as was supervision of some financial activities—but there is no less of a danger in not going far enough.

Another area with great potential to stimulate growth is trade. Think about it: 95 percent of the people in the world live outside the United States; nearly 80 percent of the world's purchasing power likewise exists beyond America's borders. Exporting is the way to reach them. The good news is that trade is a proven engine of job creation and jobs. One estimate is that every $1 billion in exports supports an estimated five thousand jobs.[2] Imports can also contribute to growth, by lowering inflation and stimulating innovation, although they also can have the effect of eliminating jobs in the short run.

The American embrace of trade has been relatively modest. The American share of global economic output is 23 percent, but its share of global exports is well below half that.[3] Another way to portray things is to point out that combined exports and imports represent some 25 percent of the US economy, compared to 62 percent for Mexico or 88 percent for Germany.[4] Exports account for only 10 million American jobs.[5]

What needs doing here? A much higher priority ought to be attached to negotiating trade agreements, preferably at the global level, but if need be regionally and bilaterally. Regional accords between the United States and Europe and the United States and Latin America are worth pursuing in addition to the already-launched efforts to bring about a free-trade zone encompassing much of the Pacific. Trade negotiations should focus not just on removing tariff and other barriers to manufactured goods, but also to reducing barriers to the export of services; promoting the free flow of agricultural goods; and reducing, or better yet, eliminating government subsidies that create playing fields anything but level. It would help if the president enjoyed Trade Promotion Authority (formerly known as Fast Track Authority), which would preclude Congress from amending, which is to say, undermining, already negotiated pacts and instead limit its role to voting yea or nay. It is also important for the United States to press other governments to allow their currencies to float freely (something that will likely weaken the dollar, thereby making US exports more competitive) and to insist on protection of American intellectual property. Dispute-resolution mechanisms should also be built into these agreements so that inevitable disagreements can be adjudicated. There is as well a close connection between building public and political support for a more open trade policy and education: Only with more of it throughout their lives will American workers be able to meet the challenges posed by ongoing technological change and global competition.

A second tool with the demonstrated potential to increase economic growth is increased investment from overseas. Opening up large amounts of American infrastructure to public-private partnerships, where a significant portion of the private funding would come from overseas, makes great sense. There may be selective situations where, for reasons of national security, foreign investment must be limited or precluded altogether, but these ought to be the exception.

Changing the way American corporations are currently taxed has the potential to make a huge difference. US corporations operate under a statutory federal tax of 35 percent of those earnings generated by activities within the United States or on profits repatriated.[6] This is a much higher rate than what is customarily imposed in the rest of the world. As might be expected, the effect is to prompt American corporations to build capacity in these other countries and to invest their profits there. Reducing the tax rates for US corporations would encourage investment of profits earned overseas in the United States, in the process creating jobs (and taxpayers) at home.

One last facet of a progrowth program deserves mention: predictability. American corporations are reportedly sitting on $1.5 to $2 trillion dollars in cash, in no small part because it is impossible to calculate a likely return on investment because so many of the factors that would determine return are uncertain. Corporations and individuals want to know about tax rates, regulation, the availability of labor, and other such factors before they make long-term decisions. They also want to be confident that the bond market will not turn against the dollar and force a rise in interest rates; this requires that the federal government make progress on reducing the deficit and remove the uncertainty inherent in frequent votes on whether to increase the debt ceiling. The sooner the government does all this, the sooner the market will get to work.

Politics

What is worth mentioning about this catalogue of problems (or challenges, if you prefer) is that none is insoluble and none exists because of a lack of resources or talent or ideas. Rather, all are man-made, or, in this case, American made. The good news is that they can be fixed. The not-so-good news is that the same reason they exist will make it hard to fix them: politics.

Will America's politics allow the United States, for more than sixty-five years the principal power in the world, to continue to play that role? The answer is anything but clear, as the gap is widening between America's internal challenges and the capacity of the country's leaders and institutions to meet them. The biggest and most immediate threat to the United States is the growing inability of the American people and the American political system to forge and sustain policies at home that will allow the country to stay strong and meet the threats (and exploit the opportunities) that will characterize the twenty-first century.

The preferred alternative would be for America's political leaders—mostly Congress and the executive branch, although governors and mayors have an important role to play as well—to agree on a plan for modernizing the country's infrastructure; reducing the deficit; improving American education; and promoting faster growth through expanded trade, increased foreign investment, and a much-revised corporate tax code. This leads to a new question: Is American politics up to the challenge? We cannot rely upon sanguine predictions that the country has worked its way through difficult challenges in the past and will do so again; to the contrary, all too much evidence suggests that the current political system is not willing and able to act, be it to reduce spending in popular entitlement programs or to increase taxes sufficiently, given the unpopularity of doing so. The causes are many, and include:

- The way congressional districts are drawn increasingly makes for "safe" Democratic and "safe" Republican seats. This allows candidates to win without needing to appeal to centrists of either party or independents, resulting in members of Congress who increasingly play out the political game closer to one or the other end zone rather than at midfield. That said, that the Senate (which in no way can be gerrymandered) is as polarized as the House of Representatives suggests that something larger is at work here. Some political scientists now speak of a "geographic sorting" of voters in which "communities and regions of the country have become more homogenous—politically, ideologically, demographically, and in terms of 'way of life.'"[1]
- Funding of politics is increasingly an individual matter. Thanks to a number of Supreme Court decisions, candidates depend much less on parties to funnel resources in their direction. Political action committees (PACs) of all sorts operate with little constraint, constituting an all but

unregulated shadow political financing system. The result is to make it more difficult to forge broad coalitions and assert influence over (much less exercise control of) more radical voices.

- Due to the explosion in the number of television channels, thanks to cable and satellite, television (as well as radio) now "narrowcasts" as much as it broadcasts. The country has come a long way since tens of millions of citizens had the common evening experience of watching one of three nightly news programs. The result is a more divided and less knowledgeable society.

- The Internet has a similar effect. Again, people tend to gravitate toward blogs and other material that reinforces their leanings and, increasingly, prejudices. Also missing is much in the way of editing or quality control over the accuracy or adequacy of information.

- More than anything else, special interests have crowded out the general interest in much of American politics. Minorities that care intensely about a specific set of issues (and whose members vote in large numbers and give money in large amounts) have far greater influence than do majorities whose commitment is limited and whose views are more nuanced. Entitlement reform, just to name one issue, is extraordinarily difficult because of the organized clout of senior citizens. The National Rifle Association has done the same to gun control. Public sector unions are one reason education reform is as tough as it is.[2]

These problems are easier to list than to resolve. It is true that America's founders designed a political process that institutionalized checks and balances, and preferred too little to too much efficiency lest the country risk sliding back into tyranny.

But the current gridlock goes far beyond what they or anyone else could have imagined, with results that are increasingly dysfunctional. We have a moved a long way away from what Alexander Hamilton argued in "Federalist No. 85": "The compacts which are to embrace thirteen distinct states in a common bond of amity and union must as necessarily be a compromise of as many dissimilar interests and inclinations."

Still, some things can and should be done. In the case of the Senate, it would make sense to ban so-called holds in which a single member can block a vote on a presidential appointment. Agreeing to schedule all votes within a set period of time would be a step forward. Far more important would be to make it more difficult to carry out filibusters in the Senate and less difficult to bring bills to the floor for debate and vote. Right now it takes a super-majority (61 votes) to cut off debate; this cedes too much blocking power to the minority. Also of use would be a reorganization of congressional committee structures to reduce overlapping jurisdictions; where that cannot be avoided, it would be a major efficiency gain for executive branch officials if Congress were to hold more joint hearings. Increasing grants of fast-track authority (which allow the executive to negotiate accords with other countries and then limit Congress to an up or down vote, rather than the right to amend, something that would force a renegotiation) would make it much less difficult for the United States to promote trade and other international agreements.

Some reforms beyond the scope of how Congress operates could also have constructive impact. Taking the power to draw congressional districts away from state legislatures and governors (and handing it to politically balanced appointed commissions) is one good idea already in effect in many states. Opening up congressional as well as presidential primaries to all voters (and not just those registered in the party) would almost certainly strengthen the hand of candidates appealing for centrist voters. Several states including California now have open, integrated primaries in which all legitimate candidates can compete.[3] A third-party movement built around set of principles designed to appeal to more conservative Democrats, more moderate Republicans, and Independents (who represent a plurality of all registered voters) could either become a serious alternative or develop ideas that the two established parties might decide to accept so as to co-opt those attracted to these positions. Increased free access to television and radio for candidates above a specified threshold of support would reduce the cost of running for office and hence reduce the need for funds; such reform makes sense regardless of whether campaign finance reform (and limiting what can be spent on campaigns) proves possible, given recent rulings of the Supreme Court. Making it easier to register and vote should strengthen the political center, as would the more radical idea of compulsory voting, something that is the law in Australia and a number of other countries. A less radical reform that would strengthen the center is the abolition of the electoral college, which among its many flaws gives disproportionate influence to a relative handful of voters in a small number of swing states and reinforces the tendency of candidates to appeal to narrow, local interests rather than approaches likely to garner broad, national support.

Notwithstanding these and other imaginable reforms, there is unlikely to be a procedural fix to what ails the country politically, if for no other reason than the very forces that have done so much to make politics difficult have made it difficult to change things, as reforms would dilute their impact and reduce their influence over issues they care passionately about. Worse yet, there are some innovations that are actually exacerbating the situation. Refusing to raise the debt ceiling, for example, prevents the government from financing programs that have already been approved and jeopardizes the government's credit rating. Particularly troubling is the increased resort to threats of severe, indiscriminate spending cuts if budget decisions aren't reached by a particular date. Artificial deadlines cannot be a substitute for a functional government process.

What is needed are real solutions if this country is to realize its potential at home and abroad. Such solutions will only emerge, however, with a president willing to make the effort to build national consensus in favor of policies opposed by strenuous minorities but supported by or acceptable to less active majorities. It also needs a revival of a culture of compromise, which would require the emergence of a small group of individuals, from both parties in the Senate and House of Representatives, who are willing to engage in the give and take integral to functional politics.[4] The alternative scenario is far less benign: continued drift and gridlock until a crisis comes along that changes the political context so that what was unthinkable yesterday becomes unavoidable today. The problem with this latter alternative is that by definition the crisis would impose terms and choices on the United States and the American people that would be far more painful and costly than what they would have to undertake if it were done voluntarily and proactively. Alas, in the absence of meaningful political reform, it is a matter of when and not whether such a crisis occurs. The only question would be the degree to which the consequences of the crisis are costly to the world and to the American people.

Conclusion

This book is premised on the idea that the world needs American leadership, but that American leadership requires the United States to first put its house in order, something that in turn will require its being more restrained in what it tries to do abroad and more disciplined in what it does at home. This is all obviously desirable. But is it doable? The short answer is yes—but doable is not the same as inevitable.

It is tempting to be glibly optimistic and quote Winston Churchill's observation, that "You can always count on Americans to do the right thing—after they've tried everything else." But this would be, well, glib. There are, to be sure, plenty of reasons for optimism: America's many excellent institutions of higher education; its relative (compared to most other countries) openness to immigrants; the availability of venture capital for promising innovations; its fundamental political stability and commitment to the rule of law; a rich endowment of minerals, energy, and water; a population that is relatively balanced in its age distribution, unlike many other developed countries that have the economic burden of a much higher percentage of elderly citizens; and the absence of a powerful "peer competitor" akin to Germany in the first half of the twentieth century and the USSR in the second.

At the same time, there are reasons for genuine concern: a debt that equals GDP and that continues to grow; persistent high unemployment, a growing percentage of which is long term; low economic growth; a K–12 educational system that is not preparing most Americans for a competitive, dynamic world; aging infrastructure; and a polarized political system that is beholden to special interests and increasingly unable to act on behalf of national interests. All this is taking place against the backdrop of a world filled with several dangerous middle-size states, a large number of actual and potential weak states, a rising China, and a host of global challenges going unmet.

The best reason for optimism is that it is possible to identify policies that will help restore American strength: reducing entitlements through raising the eligibility age, means-testing, and other reforms; revising corporate taxes so domestic spending and investment are encouraged; raising tax rates on those most able to afford them and placing a ceiling on existing tax "expenditures"; increasing energy production and cutting consumption of oil and, above all, coal through increased regulation, taxation, and shifting to other fuels; long-term deficit reduction; and doing more to expand trade and attract investment.

There also need to be changes in how the United States does things. At home, a partial list would include allowing more highly educated, talented immigrants to study and then remain in country; reforming health care so there is greater emphasis on prevention and on moving away from a system that encourages treatment and tests over results; curbing the power of public service unions and cutting back their pensions and health-care plans so they are affordable and in line with what most Americans have; creating new public-private mechanisms for funding much-needed infrastructure improvement; introducing national standards on education, improving teacher performance, and facilitating lifelong learning so that Americans will be better prepared to do well in, and adapt to, a highly competitive world.

Abroad, it would mean resisting wars of choice where the interests at stake are less than vital or where policies other than military intervention promise to yield acceptable results; cutting back on trying to transform what other countries *are* as opposed to what it is they *do*; and striving to integrate other countries into concerted efforts to strengthen weak states, rein in hostile ones, and build the international mechanisms needed to manage globalization's most pressing challenges, from encouraging trade and economic growth to thwarting climate change, pandemics, terrorism, and nuclear proliferation. Restoring priorities in the geographic sense is no less important; the Middle East has absorbed a disproportionate share of US attention and resources for too long. Asia in particular, but also Latin America, deserves a larger and more consistent place in the conduct of American foreign policy. And there is a strong case for restoring a better balance between military and nonmilitary instruments of national security.

But none of this will just happen. For the United States to stop underperforming at home, it will require real leadership, defined here as a willingness to advocate policies that are inconsistent with the narrow interests of many groups and individuals but that would be good for the society and the country as a whole. It will require leveling with the American people about the consequences of not meeting the country's challenges and what it will take to meet them. It will require taking on numerous sacred cows. It will require compromise and a degree of bipartisanship.

And for the United States to stop overreaching abroad, it will have to accept the limits to what can be accomplished and in some cases needs be accomplished. It will require setting priorities and making choices—often hard choices. It will require explaining to the American people why the government is doing what it is doing—and, implicitly, why it is not doing other things. This, too, will require real leadership.

There are three alternatives to real leadership. One is drift, which is pretty much what this country has experienced for the past decade. Business as usual, though, would likely bring about the second alternative: crisis. It could come in many forms, including an economic disaster imposed by a world that tires of lending dollars to the United States. A third alternative—faux leadership in the form of populism that would deepen social divisions without fixing problems—would be the worst of all outcomes.

It may not be realistic to do what is being called for here in these pages and survive, much less thrive, politically. It may not be possible within either of the two existing parties; it certainly won't be easy, given the twenty-first century's 24/7 Internet and media environment.

It is, however, possible. We have seen it in recent decades, in the Reagan era commission on social security, the Andrews Air Force Base budget deal agreed to by George H. W. Bush, or in the Clinton administration's success in turning a budget deficit into a surplus. The country rallied in the wake of 9/11, as it did (at least on occasion) in the aftermath of the 2008 financial crisis. We have also seen support across the political spectrum for a degree of educational reform, an increase in fuel efficiency standards, and in the introduction of a work requirement into welfare reform.

More such willingness to compromise and work across political lines is critical to America's future. Much is in the balance.

Either the United States will put its house in order and refocus what it does abroad, or it will increasingly find itself at the mercy of what happens beyond its borders and beyond its control. Such an outcome would not be in the interests of either the world or the country. The good news is that such a future can be headed off if the United States does what most Americans already know needs doing.

ACKNOWLEDGMENTS

This is the thirteenth book I have either authored or edited, and as is always the case, it reflects the contributions of many people. I want to start with Tim Bartlett. Tim is a throwback to an age when editors edited and were nothing less than full partners in the conceiving, writing, and editing of the book. Tim did not make it easy, but then that wasn't his job. He did, however, make the manuscript considerably better, for which I thank him. And while I am at it, I also want to apologize to Tim for all too often being that most tiresome of clichés, the difficult author.

Speaking of those associated with Basic Books, let me also heap praise upon Iris Bass, my copy editor. Good copyediting is not unlike a visit to the doctor: It is necessary and smart to do, but that doesn't mean it isn't also painful and humbling. Lest anyone get the wrong idea, let me just add that she was a pleasure to work with and awfully good at what she does.

I also want to give shout-outs to Annie Lenth, the project editor, who kept the many trains running on time; Kaitlyn Zafonte, Tim Bartlett's assistant, who handled the details associated with this book with considerable aplomb; Michele Jacob, the publicity director, who worked to make sure the book gathered attention rather than dust; and Lara Heimert, Basic's publisher, who was enthusiastic about and supportive of the project from the outset.

I owe a special debt to Phin Upham. After dinner with Phin and some of his colleagues in San Francisco, I managed to leave my briefcase in the car—and in the briefcase were all my notes and scribbles relating to the first draft. Phin spent most of the night tracking down

165

the car and driver, and the briefcase was back in my hands by morning. I am not sure I would have had the strength to start over.

The dictionary defines *friend* as "one attached to another by affection or esteem." All true, but my definition is somewhat different: A friend is someone who is willing to read your draft manuscript carefully and give you a candid reaction. So let me salute several wonderful friends who are equal parts generous and wise: Ted Alden, Roger Altman, Robert Blackwill, James Lindsay, Meghan O'Sullivan, and Jeffrey Reinke.

One additional reader of the manuscript merits separate and special treatment: Susan Mercandetti. Until recently, Susan was a book editor, meaning I got the benefit, which was considerable, of her professional advice. She is as good as anyone I know at helping an author frame an argument. More important, she is my wife, meaning she had to endure this author throughout the writing and editing, which as every spouse of an author can tell you, is no day at the beach. That she did it with grace and humor only adds to what I have to thank her for.

It may not take a village to write and produce a book, but it does require a few good women. In this instance, I was fortunate and then some to have Lindsay Iversen helping me with the research. Lindsay takes to heart the notion that you owe it to your boss to tell him what he needs to hear, not what he wants to. She is talented, fearless, and tireless, all of which helped to make it possible to produce what I would like to think is a good book on a tight schedule.

I also want to thank Colleen Crawford, the proverbial assistant to the assistant. Colleen was terrific in coming up with what I needed in the way of documentation and in working on the notes that fill the back of this book. Alas, she, too, has learned to speak truth to power.

Sarah Doolin, who is part of the communications shop here at the Council on Foreign Relations, gets my sincere thanks for all she did to see this book gets heard about and read. "Dooley noted" is a treat to work with.

And as always, Esther Newberg of ICM defended and looked out for me despite the gap—actually, chasm comes closer to it—in our politics and our sports loyalties.

One last item. As the book flap makes clear, my day job is being president of the Council on Foreign Relations (CFR), an independent, nonpartisan membership organization, think tank, and publisher dedicated to being a resource for its members, government officials, business executives, journalists, educators and students, civic and religious leaders, and other interested citizens in order to help them better understand the world and the foreign policy choices facing the United States and other countries. The CFR takes no institutional positions on matters of policy. All views expressed in this book are therefore my own.

This book is dedicated to Brent Scowcroft. I have known Brent for several decades. We worked as closely as two people can work together during the four years of George H. W. Bush's presidency. My prediction and conviction is that history will judge the forty-first president to be one of this country's finest, and when it does, a decent share of the credit will go to Brent Scowcroft, his national security advisor during all four of those years.

My role at the time was more modest: I was the NSC staff member responsible for overseeing the Middle East, the Persian Gulf, and South Asia. They were four extraordinary and extraordinarily busy years. The Cold War ended peacefully; a united Germany joined NATO; Iraqi aggression against Kuwait was rebuffed; the governments of Israel and the relevant Arab states met face-to-face in Madrid to talk peace. I remember one day when Brent, Bob Gates (another great public servant and Brent's deputy at the time) and I were sitting around talking, and Bob said, "I hope you guys both realize that no matter what any of us do down the road, it will never be as good as this." Bob was often right; this was no exception.

There have been more than a dozen national security advisers over the decades, but Brent is the gold standard. Somehow he managed to get the difficult balance right: representing the views of others, ensuring due process, and providing honest and wise counsel to the president. I used to tease him that was only because he got to do the job for two different presidents and had the chance to learn from his own mistakes. The real reason, though, is that Brent brought to the job both strength of character and strength of intellect.

Brent is also a gentleman, but no one should mistake his politeness for anything other than that. He has convictions (many but not all of which I share) and the courage to speak and write them (which I

NOTES

A NOTE ON SOURCES

Throughout the book, I have relied on the excellent statistical resources made available through US government agencies and nongovernmental organizations around the world.

For US debt, deficit, and GDP figures, and for data on mandatory and discretionary government expenditures, please refer to White House, Office of Management and Budget, Historical Tables, http://www.whitehouse.gov/omb/budget/Historicals, and US Department of Commerce, Bureau of Economic Analysis, "National Economic Accounts," http://www.bea.gov/national.

For data on US national security spending, please refer to White House, Office of Management and Budget, "Homeland Security Funding Analysis," Analytical Perspectives on the US Budget Fiscal Year 2013; US Department of Defense, *Overview: United States Department of Defense Fiscal Year 2013 Budget Request*, February 2012; US Department of State, *Executive Budget Summary: Function 150 and Other International Programs, Fiscal Year 2013*, February 2012; and Steven Aftergood, "Total Intelligence Budget for 2007–2009 Disclosed," Secrecy News, http://www.fas.org/blog/secrecy/2011/03/mip_disclosures.html.

For international comparisons of military spending, please refer to Stockholm International Peace Research Institute (SIPRI), "SIPRI Military Expenditure Database 2012," http://www.sipri.org/databases/milex, and European Defense Agency, "2010 Defense Data," 2011.

For statistics on energy resource production and use around the world, please refer to the many resources of the US Energy Information Administration, including its Monthly Energy Review (September 2012) and its "International Energy Statistics" database, http://www.eia.gov/cfapps/ipdbproject/IEDIndex3.cfm.

Finally, for a wide range of international economic, financial, and demographic statistics, please refer to World Bank, World DataBank, "World Development Indicators and Global Development Finance," http://databank.worldbank.org/ddp/home.do.

INTRODUCTION

1. James Warburg made a similar point in his 1944 volume that shares its title with this book. Although the country and the world faced a very different set of circumstances, Warburg argued the importance of the United States was no less clear: "We, the American people, may easily be the decisive factor in determining the future of the world . . . We are the weight which will in all probability tip the balance between a world governed by aspiration toward the four freedoms or a world governed by fear. We have not sought this decisive role, nor earned it. History has assigned it to us, and history will be written by our success or failure." —James Warburg, *Foreign Policy Begins at Home* (New York, NY: Harcourt, Brace and Co., 1944).

Part I: The Return of History

1. Francis Fukuyama, *The End of History and the Last Man* (New York, NY: Free Press, 1992).

2. C. Krauthammer, "The Unipolar Moment," *Foreign Affairs* 70, no. 1 (1990).

3. N. Birdsall and F. Fukuyama, "The Post–Washington Consensus," *Foreign Affairs* 90, no. 2 (2011).

4. Hedley Bull, *The Anarchical Society: A Study of Order in World Politics* (New York, NY: Columbia University Press, 1977).

BRAVE NEW WORLD

1. The World Bank, "Mobile Phone Access Reaches Three Quarters of Planet's Population," accessed November 26, 2012, http://www.worldbank.org/en/news/2012/07/17/mobile-phone-access-reaches

-three-quarters-planets-population; NPD Display Search, "Tablet Shipments to Surpass Notebook Shipments in 2016," accessed November 26, 2012, http://www.displaysearch.com/cps/rde/xchg/displaysearch/hs .xsl/120703_tablet_shipments_to_surpass_notebook_shipments_in _2016.asp.

2. For a further look at the geopolitical landscape, see Ian Bremmer, *Every Nation for Itself: Winners and Losers in a G–Zero World* (New York, NY: Portfolio/Penguin, 2012); George Friedman, *The Next 100 Years: A Forecast for the 21st Century* (New York, NY: Doubleday, 2009); Robert Kaplan, *The Revenge of Geography: What the Map Tells Us About Coming Conflicts and the Battle Against Fate* (New York, NY: Random House, 2012); Charles Kupchan, *No One's World: The West, the Rising Rest, and the Coming Global Turn* (New York, NY: Oxford University Press, 2012); Joseph Nye, *The Future of Power* (New York, NY: Public Affairs, 2011); and Fareed Zakaria, *The Post-American World and the Rise of the Rest* (London, England: Penguin Books, 2000).

AMERICAN PRIMACY

1. US National Intelligence Council, *Global Trends 2025: A Transformed World* (Washington, DC: US Government Printing Office, 2008). The council's analysis of the US position in the world was largely reiterated in the NIC's follow-up report. See US National Intelligence Council, *Global Trends 2030: Alternative Worlds* (Washington, DC: US Government Printing Office, 2012).

2. Carl Behrens and Carol Glover, *US Energy: Overview and Key Statistics* (Washington, DC: Congressional Research Service, April 11, 2012), R40187.

3. US Department of Defense, "Casualty Report," accessed October 4, 2012, http://www.defense.gov/NEWS/casualty.pdf.

4. Amy Belasco, *The Cost of Iraq, Afghanistan, and Other Global War on Terror Operations since 9/11* (Washington, DC: Congressional Research Service, March 29, 2011), RL33110.

5. For more on the 2003 Iraq War and the 1990 Gulf War, see Richard Haass, *War of Necessity, War of Choice: A Memoir of Two Iraq Wars* (New York, NY: Simon and Schuster, 2009).

6. US Department of Defense, "Casualty Report."

7. Belasco, *The Cost of Iraq, Afghanistan, and Other Global War on Terror Operations since 9/11*, 1.

8. Richard Haass, "We're Not Winning. It's Not Worth It," *Newsweek*, July 18, 2010.

9. R. Blackwill, "Plan B in Afghanistan," *Foreign Affairs* 90, no. 1.

10. Paul M. Kennedy, *The Rise and Fall of the Great Powers: Economic Change and Military Conflict from 1500–2000* (London: Fontana, 1989).

11. National Priorities Project, "Cost of War to the United States," accessed October 5, 2012, http://costofwar.com; Belasco, *The Cost of Iraq, Afghanistan, and Other Global War on Terror Operations since 9/11.*

12. D. Andrew Austin and Mindy Levit, *Trends in Discretionary Spending* (Washington, DC: Congressional Research Service, September 10, 2010), RL34424.

CHINA'S RISE

1. Kevin Voigt, "Now Online: Half a Billion Chinese," *CNN Business 360*, September 30, 2011, accessed November 30, 2012, http://business.blogs.cnn.com/2011/09/30/half-a-billion-china-online-internet-users.

2. US Congress, US-China Economic and Security Review Commission, Hearing on China's Internal Dilemmas, "Roots of Protest and the Party Response: Prepared Statement by Elizabeth C. Economy, C. V. Starr Senior Fellow and Director for Asia Studies, Council on Foreign Relations," First Session, 112th Congress.

3. Zheng B., "China's 'Peaceful Rise' to Great Power Status," *Foreign Affairs* 84, no. 5 (2005).

4. For further discussion of China's prospects, please see Aaron Friedberg, *A Contest for Supremacy: China, America, and the Struggle for Mastery in Asia* (New York, NY: W. W. Norton & Co., 2011); James McGregor, *No Ancient Wisdom, No Followers: The Challenges of Chinese Authoritarian Capitalism* (Westport, CT: Prospecta Press, 2012); Richard McGregor, *The Party: The Secret World of China's Communist Rulers* (New York, NY: HarperCollins Publishers, 2010); and Andrew Nathan and Andrew Scobell, *China's Search for Security* (New York, NY: Columbia University Press, 2012).

A POST-EUROPEAN WORLD

1. For example, see UK House of Lords, European Union Select Committee, "European Defence Capabilities: Lessons from the Past, Signposts for the Future," accessed December 3, 2012, http://www.publications.parliament.uk/pa/ld201012/ldselect/ldeucom/292/29204.htm.

2. Robert Gates, "The Security and Defense Agenda (Future of NATO)," (speech delivered in Brussels, Belgium, June 10, 2011), accessed November 27, 2012, http://www.defense.gov/speeches/speech.aspx?speechid=1581.

3. T. G. Ash, "The Crisis of Europe," *Foreign Affairs* 91, no. 5 (2012).

4. "Les Misérables," *The Economist,* July 28, 2012.

5. G. Carone and D. Costello, "Can Europe Afford to Grow Old?," *Finance and Development,* 43, no. 3 (2006).

THE WANNABE MAJOR POWERS

1. International Monetary Fund, "Japan: 2012 Article IV Consultation," IMF Country Report No. 12/208, August 2012.

2. For more on the issues facing modern Japan, please see Gerald Curtis, *The Logic of Japanese Politics: Leaders, Institutions, and the Limits of Change* (New York, NY: Columbia University Press, 1999) and Richard Samuels, *Securing Japan: Tokyo's Grand Strategy and the Future of East Asia* (Ithaca, NY: Cornell University Press, 2008). For more on the postwar history of Japan and its consequences for today, please see John Dower, *Embracing Defeat: Japan in the Wake of World War II* (New York, NY: W. W. Norton & Co., 1999).

3. There is much more to say about India than space allows here. For a more detailed treatment, please see Edward Luce, *In Spite of the Gods: The Rise of Modern India* (New York, NY: Anchor Books, 2008); Nandan Nilekani, *Imagining India: The Idea of a Renewed Nation* (New York, NY: Penguin Books, 2010); and Sashi Tharoor, *Pax Indica: India and the World of the 21st Century* (New York, NY: Penguin Books, 2012).

4. The geopolitical consequences of Pakistan's foreign policy extend beyond South Asia. For more details on its relationship with its neighbors and the United States, and its domestic political issues, please see Stephen P. Cohen, *The Idea of Pakistan* (Washington, DC: The Brookings Institution, 2004); Steve Coll, *Ghost Wars: The Secret History of the CIA, Afghanistan, and Bin Laden, from the Soviet Invasion to September 10, 2001* (New York, NY: Penguin Books, 2004); Pamela Constable, *Playing with Fire: Pakistan at War with Itself* (New York, NY: Random House, 2011); and Daniel Markey, *No Exit: The Future of the U.S.-Pakistan Relationship,* forthcoming.

5. Nicholas Eberstadt, "The Dying Bear," *Foreign Affairs* 90, no.6 (2011).

6. Russia's recent history has generated a number of thought-provoking books and publications, including D. Trenin et al., "The Russian Awakening," a joint paper of Carnegie Moscow Center and Carnegie Endowment for International Peace, November 2012; Thane Gustafson, *Wheel of Fortune: The Battle for Oil and Power in Russia* (Cambridge, MA: Belknap Press, 2012); Daniel Triesman, *The Return: Russia's Journey from Gorbachev to Medvedev* (New York, NY: Free Press, 2011); and Jeffrey Mankoff, *Russian Foreign Policy: The Return of Great Power Politics* (Plymouth, England: Rowman & Littlefield Publishers, Inc., 2012).

THE GLOBAL GAP

1. D. Victor, M. Morgan, J. Apt, J. Steinbruner, and K. Ricke, "The Geoengineering Option: A Last Resort Against Global Warming?," *Foreign Affairs* 88, no. 2 (2009); "Geoengineering: Rules Needed for Climate-Altering Science," *IISS Strategic Comments* 18, no. 46 (December 6, 2012).

2. Michael Walzer, *Just and Unjust Wars: A Moral Argument with Historical Illustrations* (New York, NY: Basic Books, 1977); Richard Haass, *Intervention: The Use of American Military Force in the Post–Cold War World* (Washington, DC: The Brookings Institution, 1999).

3. Daniel Drezner, "The Irony of Global Economic Governance: The System Worked," Council on Foreign Relations Working Paper, October 2012.

4. Council on Foreign Relations, *U.S. Trade and Investment Policy*, Independent Task Force Report no. 67, 2011.

5. For more on the concept and history of the failed OECD Multilateral Agreement on Investment, and its lessons for future negotiations on this issue, see E. Neumayer, "Multilateral Agreement on Investment: Lessons for the WTO from the Failed OECD Negotiations," *Wirtschaftspolitische Blätter* 46, no. 6 (1999).

6. Representatives of think tanks from around the world shared their thoughts on IMF reform in an October 2012 Council of Councils Expert Roundup, "The Case for IMF Quota Reform," accessed December 11, 2012, www.cfr.org/imf/case-imf-quota-reform/p29248.

7. The White House, "International Strategy for Cyberspace: Prosperity, Security, and Openness in a Networked World," May 2011, accessed November 28, 2012, http://www.whitehouse.gov/sites/default

/files/rss_viewer/International_Strategy_Cyberspace_Factsheet.pdf. See also Michael Gross, "World War 3.0," *Vanity Fair*, May 2012; W. Lynn III, "Defending a New Domain: The Pentagon's Cyberstrategy," *Foreign Affairs* 89, no. 5 (2010); "Internet's Future on the Agenda at Dubai Meeting," *IISS Strategic Comments* 18, no. 44 (2012); and L. Gordon Crovitz, "Would-Be Internet Regulators Need Deleting," *The Wall Street Journal*, December 10, 2012.

8. See, for example, Eric Pfanner, "Message, If Murky, from U.S. to World," *The New York Times*, December 15, 2012.

9. World Health Organization, *International Health Regulations 2005* (Geneva: World Health Organization, 2008).

10. T. Bollyky, "Developing Symptoms: Noncommunicable Diseases Go Global," *Foreign Affairs* 91, no. 3 (2012).

11. I would be remiss if I did not acknowledge the centrality of my former Brookings Institution colleagues Roberta Cohen and Francis Deng to the development of this important concept. See, in particular, Francis Deng et al., *Sovereignty as Responsibility: Conflict Management in Africa* (Washington, DC: Brookings Institution, 1996).

12. For further details, see United Nations, General Assembly, 60th Session, Resolution 60/1, "2005 World Summit Outcome," paragraphs 138–140; and United Nations, General Assembly, 63rd Session, "Implementing the Responsibility to Protect: Report of the Secretary General," January 12, 2009.

13. Kofi Annan, "My Departing Advice on How to Save Syria," *The Financial Times*, August 2, 2012.

REASON FOR OPTIMISM

1. See, for example, Steven Pinker, *The Better Angels of Our Nature: Why Violence Has Declined* (New York, NY: The Penguin Group, 2011); John Mueller, *Retreat from Doomsday: The Obsolescence of Major War* (New York, NY: Basic Books, 1989); and B. Tertrais, "The Demise of Ares: The End of War as We Know It," *The Washington Quarterly* 35, no. 3 (2012): 7–22. For a discussion of this subject with regard to American politics, see M. Zenko and M. Cohen, "Clear and Present Safety: The United States Is More Secure than Washington Thinks," *Foreign Affairs* 91, no. 2 (2012).

2. See, for example, John Mearsheimer, *The Tragedy of Great Power Politics* (New York, NY: W. W. Norton Co., 2001).

REASON FOR WORRY

1. A number of recent books, e-books, and articles capture the issues at stake with regard to Iran, including Robert Blackwill (ed.), *Iran: The Nuclear Challenge* (New York, NY: Council on Foreign Relations Press, 2012); Gideon Rose and Jonathan Tepperman (eds.), *Iran and the Bomb: Solving the Persian Puzzle* (New York, NY: Foreign Affairs, 2012); Robin Wright (ed.), *The Iran Primer: Power, Politics, and U.S. Policy* (Washington, DC: United States Institute of Peace, 2010); Abraham Sofaer, *Taking on Iran: Strength, Diplomacy, and the Iranian Threat* (New York, NY: Abraham Sofaer, 2012); and the Iran Project, "Weighing Benefits and Costs of Military Action Against Iran," September 2012, accessed December 12, 2012, http://www.wilsoncenter.org/sites/default/files/IranReport_091112_FINAL.pdf.

THE MIDDLE EAST MORASS

1. Fareed Zakaria, *The Future of Freedom: Illiberal Democracy at Home and Abroad* (New York, NY: W. W. Norton and Co., 2007).

THE CONSEQUENCES OF HISTORY'S RETURN

1. Barack Obama, interview by José Diaz-Balart, *Noticiero Telemundo*, Telemundo, September 12, 2012.

Part II: Restoration Abroad

1. To get a feel for the debate about the US role in the world, see: Andrew Bacevich, *The Limits of Power: The End of American Exceptionalism* (New York, NY: Metropolitan Books, 2010); Zbigniew Brzezinski, *Strategic Vision: America and the Crisis of Global Power* (New York, NY: Basic Books, 2012); and Robert Kagan, *The World America Made* (New York, NY: Alfred A. Knopf, 2012).

DOCTRINES AND DEMOCRACY

1. Probably the best-known scholar of "liberal peace" or "democratic peace" theory is Michael Doyle, author of *Liberal Peace: Selected Essays* (New York, NY: Routledge, 2012). For a critical perspective on the liberal peace, see Joanne Gowa, *Ballots and Bullets: The Elusive Democratic Peace* (Princeton, NJ: Princeton University Press, 1999).

2. Condoleezza Rice, "Remarks at the American University of Cairo" (speech delivered in Cairo, Egypt, June 20, 2005).

SAVING LIVES

1. James Risen, Mark Mazzetti, and Michael Schmidt, "U.S.-Approved Arms for Libya's Rebels Fell into Jihadis' Hands," *The New York Times*, December 6, 2012.

TAKING ON TERRORISTS

1. The US State Department has already begun this difficult work through its Countering Violent Extremism programs. For more information, see http://www.state.gov/j/ct/programs/index.htm. See also Ed Husain, *The Islamist: Why I Became an Islamic Fundamentalist, What I Saw Inside, and Why I Left* (London, England: Penguin Books, 2007).

2. Donald Rumsfeld, "Global War on Terrorism," October 2003, as reprinted in *USA Today*, October 16, 2003, accessed November 28, 2012, http://usatoday30.usatoday.com/news/washington/executive/rumsfeld-memo.htm.

INTEGRATION

1. I first introduced the concept of integration as a potential foreign policy doctrine in a speech to the Foreign Policy Association in New York on April 22, 2002. At the time I was director of policy planning at the Department of State. The speech can be seen here: US Department of State Archive, "Defining US Foreign Policy in a Post–Post–Cold War World," accessed on December 18, 2012, http://2001-2009.state.gov/s/p/rem/9632.htm.

RESTORATION

1. US Department of Defense, *Sustaining U.S. Global Leadership: Priorities for 21st Century Defense*, January 2012; Thomas Donlilon, "President's Asia Policy and Upcoming Trip to the Region," (speech delivered in Washington, DC at the Center for Strategic and International Studies, November 15, 2012), accessed December 12, 2012, http://csis.org/files/attachments/121511_Donilon_Statesmens_Forum_TS.pdf.

2. Robert Zoellick, "Forging Deeper Ties in the Americas," *Washington Post*, November 30, 2012.

3. Barack Obama, "Remarks by the President on the Way Forward in Afghanistan," June 22, 2011.

4. See, for example, David Sanger, *Confront and Conceal: Obama's Secret Wars and Surprising Use of American Power* (New York, NY: Crown Publishers, 2012).

A DEFENSIBLE DEFENSE

1. Amy Belasco, *The Cost of Iraq, Afghanistan, and Other Global War on Terror Operations since 9/11*, (Washington, DC: Congressional Research Service, March 29, 2011), RL33110.

2. US Department of Defense, "Sustaining U.S. Global Leadership: Priorities for 21st Century Defense," January 2012.

3. Stefan Frank, "Sec. Robert Gates in His Own Words," *Constitution Daily*, September 22, 2011, accessed December 3, 2012, http://blog.con stitutioncenter.org/2011/09/do-you-have-a-question-for-robert-gates.

4. See, for example, a study of four potential defense futures by David Barno, Nora Bensahel, and Travis Sharp, "Hard Choices: Responsible Defense in an Age of Austerity," Center for a New American Security, October 2011.

Part III: Restoration at Home

THE DEFICIT AND THE DEBT

1. Pew Fiscal Analysis Initiative, "The Great Debt Shift: Drivers of the Debt Since 2001," The Pew Charitable Trusts, April 2011, accessed December 12, 2012, http://www.pewtrusts.org/uploadedFiles/www pewtrustsorg/Fact_Sheets/Economic_Policy/drivers_federal_debt_ since_2001.pdf.

2. R. Haass and R. Altman, "American Profligacy and American Power: The Consequences of Fiscal Irresponsibility," *Foreign Affairs* 89, no. 6 (2010).

3. For a more detailed discussion of available Social Security reform options, see David John and Virginia Reno, "Perspectives: Options for Reforming Social Security," AARP Public Policy Institute, accessed December 12, 2012, http://www.aarp.org/content/dam/aarp/research /public_policy_institute/econ_sec/2012/compilation-of-options -social-security-AARP-ppi-health.pdf.

4. Centers for Medicare and Medicaid Services, "National Health Expenditure Projections 2011–2021," 2011; Jason Kane, "Health Costs: How the U.S. Compares with Other Countries," *The Rundown*, PBS NewsHour, October 22, 2012.

5. For extended discussion of these issues, please see David Brown, Gabe Horwitz, and David Kendall, "Necessary but Not Sufficient:

Why Taxing the Wealthy Can't Fix the Deficit," and "Death by a Thousand Cuts: Why Spending Cuts Alone Won't Fix the Deficit," Third Way, September, 2012; Martin Feldstein, "How to Cut the Deficit Without Raising Taxes," *Washington Post*, November 29, 2010; US Congress, Congressional Budget Office, "Effects of Adopting a Value Added Tax," February, 1992; and Josh Barro, "Value-Added Tax Would Raise Tons for U.S. Coffers," *Bloomberg*, May 2, 2012.

6. The National Commission on Fiscal Responsibility and Reform, "The Moment of Truth," December 2010.

ENERGY

1. For background, see Daniel Yergin, *The Quest: Energy, Security, and the Remaking of the Modern World* (New York, NY: Penguin Books, 2012).

2. International Energy Agency, "World Energy Outlook 2012," November 12, 2012, accessed December 12, 2012, http://www.world energyoutlook.org/publications/weo-2012/#d.en.26099.

3. For a summary of the new rules, see Bill Vlasic, "U.S. Sets Much Higher Fuel Efficiency Standards," *The New York Times*, August 28, 2012. For a detailed explanation of the regulations, see United States National Archives and Records Administration, Federal Register, vol. 77, no. 199, pp. 62623–63200, accessed December 12, 2012, http://www.nhtsa.gov/fuel-economy.

4. T. Boone Pickens has been highlighting the potential of natural gas for several years. See, for example, Alex Kowalski, "Trucks Run on Natural Gas in Pickens Clean Energy Drive: Freight," *Bloomberg*, accessed November 28, 2012, http://www.bloomberg.com/news/2012–02–29 /trucks-run-on-natural-gas-in-pickens-clean-energy-drive.html.

5. State Budget Crisis Task Force, "Report of the State Budget Crisis Task Force," July 31, 2012; US Congress, Congressional Budget Office, "How Would Proposed Fuel Economy Standards Affect the Highway Trust Fund?," May 2012, and US Department of Transportation, Federal Highway Administration, "Financing Federal-Aid Highways," accessed on December 18, 2012, http://www.fhwa.dot.gov/reports /fifahiwy/fifahio5.htm.

6. Nuclear Energy Institute, "Resources and Stats: U.S. Nuclear Power Plants," accessed November 28, 2012, http://www.nei.org/resources andstats/nuclear_statistics/usnuclearpowerplants.

7. Charles Ferguson, *Nuclear Energy: Balancing Risks and Benefits* (New York, NY: Council on Foreign Relations, April, 2007), Council Special Report No. 28.

EDUCATION

1. Sam Dillon, "Top Test Scores from Shanghai Stun Educators," *The New York Times*, December 7, 2010, accessed September 7, 2012, http://www.nytimes.com/2010/12/07/education/07education.html.

2. Council on Foreign Relations, *U.S. Education Reform and National Security*, Independent Task Force Report No. 68, 2012. Unless otherwise cited, basic statistics in this section are derived from this report.

3. Huffington Post, "Education: U.S. Graduation Rate, Unemployment Compared to Other Nations in Infographic," June 26, 2012, accessed September 7, 2012, http://www.huffingtonpost.com/2012/06/26/infographic-shows-how-us-_n_1628187.html.

4. Mark Dixon, "Public Education Finances: 2010," US Census Bureau, June 2012, Figs. 2 and 6.

5. Organisation for Economic Co-operation and Development (OECD), *Education at a Glance 2011: OECD Indicators*, OECD Publishing, 2011, accessed September 7, 2012, http://dx.doi.org/10.1787/eag-2011-en.

6. Jeff Smink, "This Is Your Brain on Summer," *The New York Times*, July 27, 2011.

7. For more on the Common Core standards, see http://www.corestandards.org.

8. US Department of Labor, Bureau of Labor Statistics, "Employment Situation Summary," November 2, 2012, accessed November 28, 2012, http://www.bls.gov/news.release/empsit.nro.htm.

9. M. Spence, "Globalization and Unemployment: The Downside of Integrating Markets," *Foreign Affairs* 90, no. 4 (2011).

10. Deloitte, Manufacturing Institute, "Boiling Point? The Skills Gap in U.S. Manufacturing," 2011; Richard Haass and Klaus Kleinfeld, "Lack of Skilled Employees Hurting Manufacturing," *USA Today*, July 3, 2012; Chris Bryant, "A German Model Goes Global," *Financial Times*, May 21, 2012.

INFRASTRUCTURE

1. American Society of Civil Engineers, "Report Card for America's Infrastructure," accessed November 28, 2012, http://www.infrastructure reportcard.org.

2. State Budget Crisis Task Force, "Report of the State Budget Crisis Task Force," July 31, 2012; US Department of Transportation, Federal Highway Administration, "Financing Federal-Aid Highways," accessed on December 18, 2012, http://www.fhwa.dot.gov/reports/fifahiwy /fifahio5.htm.

3. Council on Foreign Relations, "Road to Nowhere: Federal Transportation Infrastructure Policy: Progress Report and Scorecard," June 2012.

4. American Society of Civil Engineers, "Fact Sheet: Roads," accessed November 28, 2012, http://www.infrastructurereportcard.org /fact-sheet/roads.

5. CFR, "Road to Nowhere"; PolitiFact Ohio, "Rep. Tim Ryan Says China and India Outspend U.S. on Infrastructure," August 9, 2011, accessed November 28, 2012, http://www.politifact.com/ohio/statements /2011/aug/09/tim-ryan/rep-tim-ryan-says-china-and-india-outspend -us-infr.

IMMIGRATION

1. For an insightful look at US immigration policy since 9/11, see Edward Alden, *The Closing of the American Border: Terrorism, Immigration, and Security Since 9/11* (New York, NY: Harper Collins, 2008). For a recent assessment of immigration reform options, see Council on Foreign Relations, *U.S. Immigration Policy*, Independent Task Force Report No. 69, 2009.

2. National Commission on Terrorist Attacks upon the United States, "Staff Statement No. 1: Entry of the 9/11 Hijackers into the United States," accessed September 12, 2012, http://govinfo.library.unt .edu/911/staff_statements/staff_statement_1.pdf.

3. Shannon O'Neil, *Two Nations Indivisible: Mexico, the United States, and the Road Ahead* (New York: Oxford University Press, 2013); Jeffrey Passel, D'Vera Cohn, and Ana Gonzalez-Barrera, "Net Migration from Mexico Falls to Zero—and Perhaps Less," Pew Hispanic Center, Pew Research Center, May 3, 2012.

4. See, for example, Dov S. Zakheim, "Immigration Policy Is Foreign Policy," *The National Interest*, November 14, 2012.

5. US Department of Homeland Security, *2011 Yearbook of Immigration Statistics*, 2012, 18, Table 6: Persons Obtaining Legal Permanent Resident Status by Type and Major Class of Admission: FY 2002–2011.

6. Department of Homeland Security, "Characteristics of H-1B Specialty Occupation Workers: Fiscal Year 2011 Annual Report to Congress, October 1, 2010–September 30, 2011," U.S. Citizenship and Immigration Services, March 12, 2012.

7. For more on these issues, see Associated Press, "Visa Issue Spurs Microsoft Office in Canada," accessed November 28, 2012, http://www.msnbc.msn.com/id/19619896/ns/technology_and_science-tech_and_gadgets/t/visa-issue-spurs-microsoft-office-canada/#.UJvkdz1oFyI; U.S. Chamber of Commerce and Immigration Policy Center, "Immigrant Entrepreneurs—Creating Jobs and Strengthening the Economy," January 2012; Partnership for a New American Economy, "The 'New American' Fortune 500," June 2011; Vivek Wadhwa, AnnaLee Saxenian, Ben Rissing, and Gary Gereffi, "America's New Immigrant Entrepreneurs," Duke University and the University of California at Berkeley, June 2007; Council on Foreign Relations, *U.S. Immigration Policy*, Independent Task Force Report No. 63, 2009; and B. Lindsay Lowell, Julia Gelatt, and Jeanne Batalova, "Immigrants and Labor Force Trends: The Future, Past, and Present," *MPI Insight*, No. 17, July 2006.

ECONOMIC GROWTH

1. There is an increasingly robust debate about prospects for US economic growth. On one side are those who argue that a number as high as 4 percent is possible. See, for example, Brendan Miniter (ed.), *The 4% Solution: Unleashing the Economic Growth America Needs* (New York, NY: Crown Business, 2012). On the other side of the debate are those who project a rate of growth that could be as low as 1 to 1.5 percent. See, for example, Jason Zweig, "US Stocks: Look Out Below?" *The Wall Street Journal*, December 15, 2012.

2. Office of the United States Trade Representative, "Benefits of Trade," accessed October 19, 2012, http://www.ustr.gov/about-us/benefits-trade.

3. US Department of Agriculture, Economic Research Service, "Real Historical GDP Shares and Growth Rates of GDP Shares for

Baseline Countries/Regions (in percent) 1969–2011," January 26, 2012; World Trade Organization, *International Trade Statistics 2011*, 24, table 1.8.

4. Organisation for Economic Co-operation and Development (OECD), *National Accounts at a Glance 2011*, December 2011.

5. US Department of Commerce, International Trade Administration, "Exports Support American Jobs," International Trade Research Report No. 1, April 2010.

6. Jane Gravelle, *International Corporate Tax Rate Comparisons and Policy Implications* (Washington, DC: Congressional Research Service, March 31, 2011), R41743. For ideas on how to improve the taxation climate for business, see Robert Pozen, "How to Tax Foreign Profits of U.S. Companies," *Financial Times*, February 23, 2012.

POLITICS

1. James Thomson, "A House Divided: Polarization and Its Effect on RAND," RAND Corporation, 2010, accessed November 29, 2012, http://www.rand.org/pubs/occasional_papers/OP291.

2. Mancur Olson's classic remains the finest analysis of this dynamic. See Mancur Olson, *The Rise and Decline of Nations: Economic Growth, Stagflation, and Social Rigidities* (New Haven, CT: Yale University Press, 1982). See also Jonathan Rauch, *Demosclerosis* (New York, NY: Times Books, 1994).

3. Mickey Edwards, *The Parties Versus the People: How to Turn Republicans and Democrats into Americans* (New Haven, CT: Yale University Press, 2012).

4. Centrist organizations such as Third Way and the Bipartisan Policy Center, by creating a platform for dialogue and compromise, have important roles to play in this regard. Michael Gerson, writing recently in the *Washington Post*, argued that leadership will be necessary to make the changes needed for more trying economic times. See Michael Gerson, "Wanted: Leaders for Lean Times," *Washington Post*, November 30, 2012.

INDEX